THE
50
MOST MYSTERIOUS PLACES EVER

TEXT BY BRIAN FRESCHI – ILLUSTRATIONS BY DOMENICO RUSSO

whitestar*kids

CONTENTS

This journey around the world stops at the 50 most mysterious
places on the planet.
Are you ready
to go on an adventure?

1 Stonehenge (Great Britain) .... *page* **8**

2 Loch Ness (Great Britain) .... *page* **10**

3 Fingal's Cave (Great Britain) .... *page* **12**

4 San Juan de Gaztelugatxe (Spain) .... *page* **13**

5 Quinta da Regaleira (Portugal) .... *page* **14**

6 Alchemical Caves (Italy) .... *page* **15**

7 Gardens of Bomarzo (Italy) .... *page* **16**

8 Carnac Stones (France) .... *page* **18**

9 Paris Catacombs (France) .... *page* **20**

10 Devil's Bridge (Germany) .... *page* **22**

11 Black Forest (Germany) .... *page* **24**

12 Crooked Forest (Poland) .... *page* **25**

13 Hessdalen Lights and Aurora Borealis (Scandinavia) .... *page* **26**

14 Hoia Baciu Forest (Romania) .... *page* **28**

15 Krudum Hill (Czech Republic) .... *page* **30**

16 Buda Castle Labyrinth (Hungary) .... *page* **32**

17 Dargavs (Russia) .... *page* **34**

18 Mammoth Bone Buildings (Ukraine and Russia) .... *page* **35**

19 Tunnel of Love (Ukraine) .... *page* **36**

20 Pamukkale Thermal Pools (Turkey) .... *page* **38**

21 Giza Necropolis (Egypt) .... *page* **40**

22 Eye of the Sahara (Mauritania) .... *page* **42**

23 Fairy Circles (Namibia) .... *page* **44**

24 Gates of Hell (Turkmenistan) .... *page* **46**

25 Vaitheeswaran Koil (India) .... *page* **48**

26 North Sentinel Island (India) .... *page* **50**

27 Heizhugou Forest (China) .... *page* **52**

28 Terracotta Army (China) .... *page* **54**

29 Genghis Khan's Grave (Mongolia) .... *page* **56**

30 Mysterious Road (South Korea) .... *page* **58**

31 Ise Shrine (Japan) .... *page* **60**

32 Plain of Jars (Laos) .... *page* **62**

33 Marine Bioluminescence (Maldives) .... *page* **64**

34 Slope Point (New Zealand) .... *page* **66**

35 Devil's Sea (Pacific Ocean) .... *page* **68**

36 Mariana Trench (Pacific Ocean) .... *page* **69**

37 Abraham Lake (Canada) .... *page* **70**

38 Bermuda Triangle (Atlantic Ocean) .... *page* **71**

39 Area 51 (USA) .... *page* **72**

40 Sailing Stones at Racetrack Playa (USA) .... *page* **74**

41 Naica Mine (Mexico) .... *pagc* **76**

42 Island of the Dead Dolls (Mexico) .... *page* **78**

43 Snake Island (Brazil) .... *page* **80**

44 Enchanted Well (Brazil) .... *page* **82**

45 Catatumbo Lightning (Venezuela) .... *page* **84**

46 Uyuni Salt Flat (Bolivia) .... *page* **86**

47 El Ojo, the Rotating Island (Argentina) .... *page* **88**

48 Nazca Lines (Peru) .... *page* **90**

49 Machu Picchu (Peru) .... *page* **92**

50 Easter Island (Chile) .... *page* **94**

ARCTIC
OCEAN

ASIA

14

19

17

24

18

20

21

29

27

28

30

31

PACIFIC
OCEAN

32

25

26

35

36

33

INDIAN
OCEAN

AUSTRALIA

34

LET'S GO!

STONEHENGE

· GREAT BRITAIN ·
Salisbury Plain, Wiltshire County, Southern England
Built Between 3100 BCE and 1600 BCE

"Higher, higher. Wait, go right, a little more, a little more, perfect." This is how we like to imagine the Britons as they positioned GIANT STONES weighing between 3 and 20 tons to give rise to one of humanity's most hotly debated sites: Stonehenge. **Too bad they forgot to leave us the instruction booklet because the purpose of this ring of megaliths is still unknown.**

"Star-obsessed Druid nerds built it!" said antiquarian John Aubrey in 1640.

"Those Druids were better scientists than me," thought an embarrassed Isaac Newton.

"No, it's from the Bronze Age! Look at this bowl found nearby," exclaimed archaeologist John Lubbock in 1840.

Stonehenge was built in stages over the millennia, and some of the very heavy boulders appear to have been originally transported from Wales, a good 150 miles (240 km) away. **The "how" weighs heavy on the mystery!**

Some say it was once an astronomical observatory because of its alignment with the sun during the solstices, others say it was a necropolis for important figures, and some say it was a cultural center for priests.

Only one thing is certain: they're more than simple rocks!

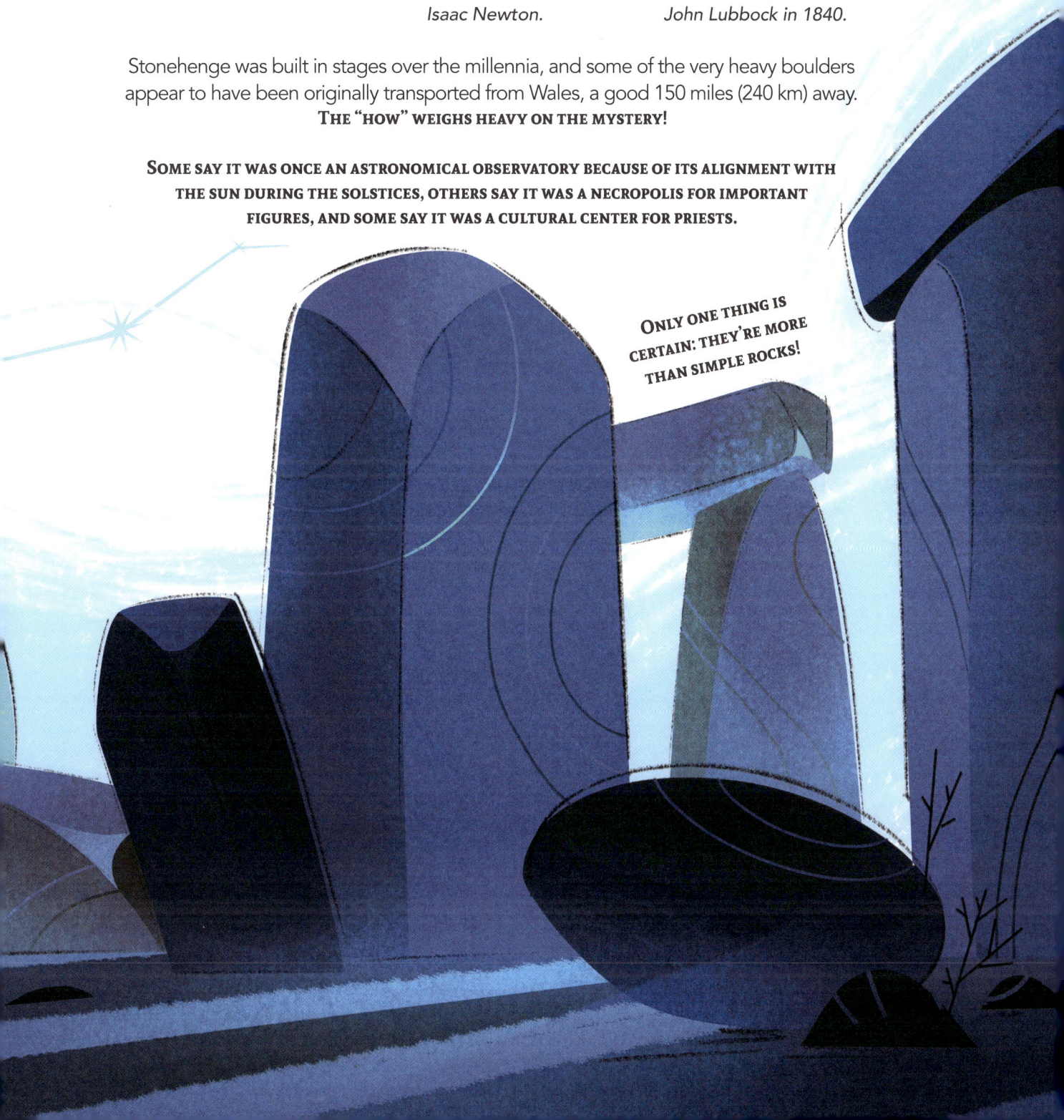

LOCH NESS

· GREAT BRITAIN ·
Scottish Highlands, Southwest of Inverness
Length: 23 miles (37 km) – Maximum Depth: 755 feet (230 m)

You're now in a small boat on the murky water of one of the world's most famous lakes. You have a simple mission: to prove the existence of a LEGEND that's more than 1,000 years old!

What legend? Nessie, of course!
Grab your camera before...
Oh, nevermind, it's just a twig.

Formed 10,000 years ago during the last glacial period, Loch Ness contains more water than all the lakes in England and Wales combined. However, what it's known for is the incredible creature that seems to live in its depths, attracting hordes of tourists and alien fans (obviously).

Just think! The first sighting occurred in 565 CE, by the Irish monk Saint Columba: *"We need a boat! Go on, swim to the other shore and get it!"* he told one of his fellow travelers. Too bad that, as legend has it, the poor guy was grabbed by something in the water: a monster!

In 1933, a couple told a local newspaper that they had seen a prehistoric animal right near the lake, while in 1934, physician Robert Kenneth Wilson published the photograph that made Nessie the most famous plesiosaur of the time. Except that it was a toy submarine!

PERHAPS SHE'S HIDING IN A CAVE? PERHAPS SHE'S ACTUALLY AN EEL? HOW COULD A DINOSAUR LIVE 70 MILLION YEARS? SO MANY UNANSWERED QUEST... WHOAAA!

THERE SHE IS!
NO, THAT'S ANOTHER TWIG...

FINGAL'S CAVE

· GREAT BRITAIN ·
Staffa Island, Inner Hebrides
Size: 280 feet (85 m) with a vaulted ceiling of 65 feet (20 m)

And if I told you that works of art and musical compositions were inspired not only by cheesy love stories but also by... CAVES?
That's true of Fingal's Cave, a sea cave discovered in 1772 by naturalist Joseph Banks, named after Fingal Mac Cumhaill, a hero who, according to legend, built a path to connect Scotland and Ireland!

This cave was created 60 million years ago by a lava flow that hardened into hexagonal forms, creating enormous columns, and when the waves penetrate its walls, they produce enigmatic echoes!
Indeed, the cave is called Uamh-Binn, which in Gaelic means "cave of melody."

For centuries, this mystery not only influenced painters and composers...

...it also attracted many important visitors, such as writer Jules Verne, the musicians of Pink Floyd, and even Queen Victoria!

SAN JUAN DE GAZTELUGATXE

· SPAIN ·
BISCAY PROVINCE, BASQUE COUNTRY
LENGTH: 2.1 MILES (3.4 KM) – CHANGE IN ALTITUDE: 755 FEET (286 M)

San Juan de Gaztelugatxe (now say that five times quickly) is an island surrounded by the Cantabrian Sea and Mount Burgoa and connected to the mainland by a 14th-century bridge!

WALK, WALK SOME MORE, AND, 260 FEET (80 M) ABOVE SEA LEVEL AND AFTER A NARROW PATH WITH OVER 230 STEPS, THERE YOU ARE, IN FRONT OF THE SMALL 10TH-CENTURY HERMITAGE DEDICATED TO SAINT JOHN THE BAPTIST.

Can you imagine? Over the centuries, it has changed a lot due to wars, fires, and looting by corsairs, and has even been used as a prison for women accused of WITCHCRAFT!

IF YOU SURVIVED THE LONG CLIMB, BE SURE TO RING THE BELL THREE TIMES... IT IS SAID TO MAKE WISHES COME TRUE!

QUINTA DA REGALEIRA

· PORTUGAL ·
CITY OF SINTRA, IN THE METROPOLITAN AREA OF LISBON
CONSTRUCTION: BETWEEN 1904 AND 1911 – DEPTH: 88 FEET (27 M)

Did you know that there is a waterless well in Portugal that seems to be thousands of years old but was only built in the early 1900s by an eccentric (and very rich) MASON!?

IT'S THE INITIATORY WELL AT QUINTA DA REGALEIRA, AN ENORMOUS ESTATE THAT'S COVERED BY GARDENS, PALACES, LAKES, FOUNTAINS, LABYRINTHINE CAVES... AND PEPPERED WITH MYSTERIOUS AND ESOTERIC SYMBOLS!

The land belonged to a businessman named Carvalho Monteiro, who, with the help of architect Luigi Manini, created a really crazy place to express his love of Gothic, Roman, Renaissance, and just about any other architectural style you can think of! The Poço Iniciàtico stands out: this "Initiation Well" looks like an upside-down tower. It is marked by symbols everywhere and has a spiral staircase, 23 small side niches, a stone compass in the shape of a Templar cross at the bottom, and four underground tunnels!

MONTEIRO WAS ALMOST CERTAINLY AN INITIATE OF THE KNIGHTS TEMPLAR, A MEDIEVAL CATHOLIC ORDER, AND MANY THINK THE WELL WAS THE STAGE FOR RITUALS FILLED WITH BLINDFOLDED PEOPLE AND SWORDS!

ALCHEMICAL CAVES

· ITALY ·

TURIN

CONSTRUCTION: 9TH CENTURY

What if I told you that you can visit three damp, dark places full of magical mysteries that may not really exist? JUST KIDDING! You can't... I have piqued your interest, though. Admit it!

ACCORDING TO LEGEND, UNDERNEATH THE CITY OF TURIN, THERE ARE THREE ALCHEMICAL CAVES THAT CONNECT DIFFERENT CHURCHES AND PALACES. THEY'RE THE KIND OF PLACE WHERE ALCHEMISTS WENT TO CHAT ABOUT CHEMISTRY AND ASTROLOGY ON THEIR COFFEE BREAK. TOO BAD THAT NO ONE KNOWS WHERE THEY ARE!

According to experts, the first cave is the size of a cart and actually was used by rulers as a secret room, while the second may even lead all the way to the Church of Gran Madre di Dio, where a shadowy Egyptian cult apparently gathered. The third, on the other hand, is said to contain the very famous philosopher's stone, a talisman that could grant people eternal life and turn hum-drum metals into gold!

WHAT IF THEY WERE PORTALS TO PARALLEL WORLDS? COULD BE...

15

GARDENS OF BOMARZO

· ITALY ·

Province of Viterbo
Construction: 1547

Tired of all these trips, you've decided to spend a leisurely afternoon at an amusement park, even if it doesn't quite look like the one you saw on the poster.
To begin with, there's no roller coaster.
And...it's full of MONSTERS!

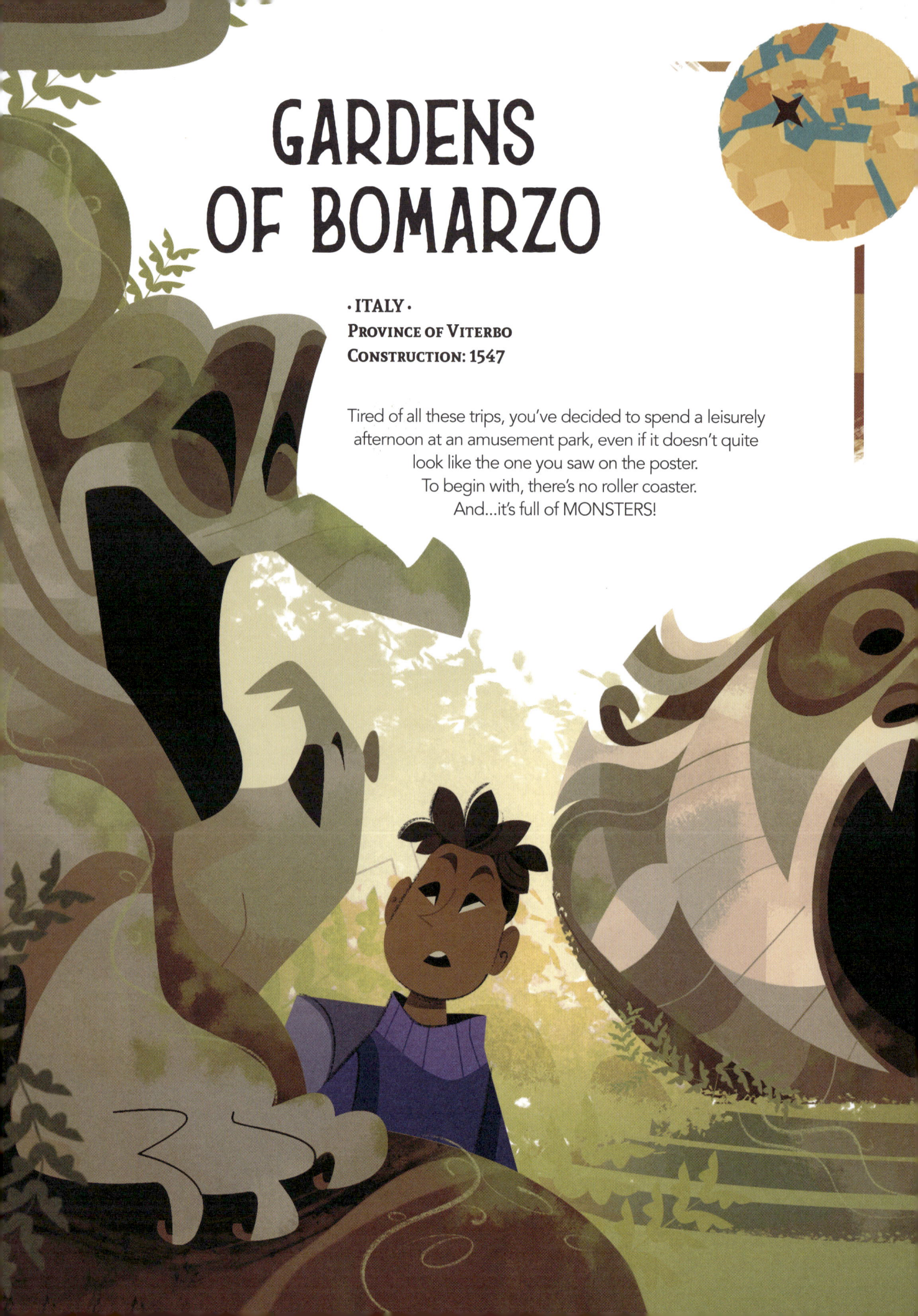

Well, it looks like you took a wrong turn again and have ended up in the Gardens of Bomarzo, a.k.a. Park of the Monsters!
It all began when Prince Vicino Orsini commissioned architect Pirro Ligorio and sculptor Simone Moschino to make numerous statues and basalt structures to lessen his grief over the loss of Giulia Farnese, his beloved wife.
They created the "Sacred Forest," a labyrinth of animals and deities immersed in a forest of conifers and deciduous trees, with a dash of mythology and alchemy for good measure!
THE STATUES VARY IN SIZE AND MANY OF THEM ARE ENGRAVED WITH ENIGMATIC INSCRIPTIONS THAT MANY SCHOLARS ARE STILL SCRATCHING THEIR HEADS OVER.

So, let's kick off the tour! Sphinxes, nymphs, dolphins, elephants with Roman legionnaires clutched in their trunks, wyverns (sort of like small dragons), giants hitting each other, turtles and whales staring at each other, scary ogres with their mouths wide open, tilted houses that make you lose your balance...
There's so much you lose count!

AND TO THINK THAT AFTER THE PRINCE'S DEATH, THE PARK WAS ABANDONED FOR 400 YEARS! IT WAS RESTORED ONLY IN THE MID-1900s.

NOT BAD, NOT BAD. MAYBE EVEN BETTER THAN A FERRIS WHEEL!

CARNAC STONES

· FRANCE ·

Lorient, in the Department of Brittany

Construction: 5th–3rd millennium BCE

You're in the French countryside and you feel like you've been here before. It's as if you've already seen and photographed all these huge STONES, which stretch out as far as the eye can see! Maybe drinking too many fizzy drinks has done a number on your memory! Nahhh, it's just that you're in Carnac, surrounded by its mysterious megalithic "alignments." Sort of like those at Stonehenge!

INDIVIDUAL MENHIRS (STANDING STONES) AND CLUSTERS OF STONES CALLED DOLMENS STRETCH FOR MILES BETWEEN THE KERMARIO, KERLESCAN, AND MÉNEC AREAS, REACHING A NUMBER OF ABOUT 3,000 MEGALITHS ARRANGED IN ROWS AND FANS! ONE OF THEM IS ALSO THE WORLD'S LARGEST MENHIR, AT 65 FEET (20 M) AND 330 TONS (300 METRIC TONS) OF SOLID ROCK!

That's all very well and good, but no one knows who erected them or why! Certain arrangements really resemble the shape of a temple, so perhaps they were used as religious sites or to bury famous people. Like Julius Caesar, at war with the Celts...
Not to mention that, according to legend, those rocks are really Roman legions turned to stone!

BUT DON'T BE SILLY! THESE MEGALITHS ARE MUCH OLDER!

Well, then maybe they were built by the hunter-gatherers who lived in the area. They were so adventurous that they even knew about whales and drew hem on the stones!

LET THE DEBATE ABOUT
THE STONES BEGIN!

PARIS CATACOMBS

· FRANCE ·

PARIS, ENTRANCE AT PLACE DENFERT-ROCHEREAU – INAUGURATION: APRIL 7, 1786

SKELETONS, skeletons everywhere! And they aren't the nice glow-in-the-dark kind, like the ones you hang on Halloween. They are real and really scary!
RUN AS FAST AS YOU CAN TO THE FLIGHT OF STEPS THAT LEADS TO A LIGHT... You've REACHED THE GIFT SHOP, SAFE AND SOUND!

One thing is certain: you'll never visit the Paris Catacombs alone again!

Also known as the Empire of the Dead, the catacombs are 65 to 100 feet deep (20 to 30 m) and hold the remains of roughly 6 million people. It all started in the late 1700s, when Les Innocents and all the other local parish cemeteries were closed. The reason was simple: people had been buried in mass graves for centuries and there was no more room! This caused a whole lot of problems, from illnesses (much worse than your average cold) to neighbors complaining about the stench.

So, they loaded all the bones onto large wagons and, at night, between 1786 and 1814, they moved them to the old quarries under Paris, which were hundreds of miles long and abandoned after they had caused several roads to cave in. In 1809, some parts of the catacombs were opened for the macabre and mystery-loving public. Even Napoleon took a tour of them!

Are you wondering why the only bones you see are skulls, legs, and arms? Well, that's because the others were used to renovate the damaged walls!

How scary!

DEVIL'S
BRIDGE

· GERMANY ·

RHODODENDRON PARK, KRUMLAU-GABLENZ, SAXONY
CONSTRUCTION: BETWEEN 1866 AND 1875

Did you know that there are dozens of perfectly arched bridges
that are said to have been built by the DEVIL himself!? No?
Well, let me tell you another secret...
You are standing right on top of one! Surprise!

THE RAKOTZBRÜCKE IS LOCATED IN KROMLAU, A PARK OFTEN PHOTOGRAPHED
BY FLOWER LOVERS FOR ITS BEAUTIFUL RHODODENDRONS. THE LOCAL TOWN'S
KNIGHT, HERRMANN FRIEDRICH RÖTSCHKE, HAD A MYSTERIOUS
ARCHITECT BUILD IT SO THAT PEOPLE COULD PASS FROM ONE SIDE
OF THE RAKOTZSEE LAKE TO THE OTHER.

At 65 feet (20 m) long and anchored by basalt columns on each side, this bridge is not only super impressive, it's also capable of creating a perfect circle when reflected in the water below. That, of course, has given rise to a myriad of funny and spooky legends!

Some people think the circle is a portal to another dimension, while others claim that if you pass under it during the full moon you'll get superpowers! But the best legends are really the ones about the Devil! The most popular tale tells of a pact between the Devil and an architect. *"My friend!"* said the Devil. *"I will build a perfect bridge for you, and in return I want the soul of the first person to cross it."* But the man was quite clever and he let a dog pass first, fooling the demon!

Evidently he was a cat guy.

BLACK FOREST

·GERMANY·
State of Baden-Württemberg
Size: 2,320 square miles (6,009 sq km)

Fog, witches, monasteries, fortresses, WEREWOLVES...
No, I'm not talking about the latest fantasy-themed writing assignment your teacher gave you as homework. I'm talking about the Black Forest! Called "Black" because of the endless expanses of fir and beech trees, this forest is a mountainous area that is home to breathtaking views, quaint villages, delicious desserts, and even centuries-old legends!

Like Schlossberg, the hill where ghosts hide in the trees, or Mummelsee, a lake with early-bird mermaids who will try to capture you (yes, apparently there are freshwater mermaids too!).
But the ghosts of the two evil monks of St. Blaise Abbey are no joke either. Good thing a Capuchin monk was able to catch them and throw them off the Feldberg, the highest mountain in the area.

This forest is so mysterious that some Brothers Grimm fairy tales, like Little Red Riding Hood and Hansel and Gretel, are set precisely here!

CROOKED FOREST

· POLAND ·

VILLAGE OF NOWE CZARNOWO, WEST POMERANIAN VOIVODESHIP
SIZE: 1.25 ACRES (0.5 HECTARES)

Are you tired of doing the exact same things over and over?
Breakfast at the same time, school at the same time,
homework at the same time, every day.
Wouldn't CHANGE be nice every once in a while?
THAT'S EXACTLY WHAT THE SCOTS PINES IN THE FOREST NEAR THE TOWN OF GRYFINO THOUGHT WHEN THEY DECIDED TO TWIST AND TURN AS THEY GREW! PLANTED IN THE 1930S, TODAY THERE ARE ABOUT 100 OR SO OF THEM LEFT. THEY'RE SO INCREDIBLE DUE TO THEIR SHAPE: THEIR TRUNKS ARE BENT 90 DEGREES TO THE NORTH, ABOUT 4–20 INCHES (10–50 CM) ABOVE THE GROUND, THEN THEY CURVE ANYWHERE FROM 3 TO 10 FEET (1 TO 3 M) BEFORE GROWING UPWARD AGAIN.

They basically look like upside-down question marks!
The best thing about them? No one knows why! The leading theory
is that someone trained them to grow that way while they were
young because arched wood is useful for building chairs,
ships, or sleds!

*SOME EVEN SAY IT WAS WORLD WAR II
TANKS THAT CRUSHED THEM OR SNOWSTORMS
THAT BENT THEM!*

HESSDALEN LIGHTS AND AURORA BOREALIS

· SCANDINAVIA ·

HESSDALEN LIGHTS: NORWAY, ABOUT 60 MILES (100 KM) SOUTHEAST OF TRONDHEIM
AURORA BOREALIS: NORTHERN HEMISPHERE

You know that LASER pointer you got for your birthday that you point at the wall to drive your cat crazy? What if I told you that something similar also happens in nature and that it drives people (rather than cats) crazy too!

IN THE VALLEY NEAR THE VILLAGE OF HESSDALEN, THE LOCALS HAVE SEEN WEIRD GEOMETRICALLY SHAPED LIGHTS FLOATING IN THE SKY SINCE THE 1930S! SOMETIMES THEY LAST A FEW SECONDS, SOMETIMES HOURS ON END! SOMETIMES THEY MOVE SLOWLY, SOMETIMES THEY DART AND FLASH ABOUT RANDOMLY. THEY CAN BE AS BIG AS CARS; ALONE OR IN GROUPS; WHITE, BLUE, OR RED... AND ACCOMPANIED BY NUMEROUS FLASHES IN THE SKY!

The kind of stuff that will really blow your mind!
The Hessdalen Lights have always made physicists around the world anxious!

"They're formed through the combustion of airborne dust!"

"No! They're caused by the decay of chemical elements!"

"You've got it all wrong! They're natural batteries created thanks to metal minerals combined with sulfur-filled water!"

In short, it almost came to blows!
But in Scandinavia, light phenomena aren't that rare.
JUST THINK OF THE AURORA BOREALIS! A CRAZY MIX OF BANDS OF LIGHT OCCURRING IN A HUGE RING-SHAPED AREA CALLED THE AURORAL OVAL. THE RECIPE TO CREATE THESE NORTHERN LIGHTS IS VERY SIMPLE: THE SUN'S MEGA-EXPLOSIONS GIVE OFF ENERGY PARTICLES THAT ARE PUSHED TOWARD THE EARTH'S NORTH AND SOUTH POLES. THEY GAIN AN ELECTRIC CHARGE AND RUN INTO ATOMS AND GAS MOLECULES IN THE ATMOSPHERE, RESULTING IN BURSTS OF COLOR!

Actually, this phenomenon isn't exclusive to Earth. It happens on Jupiter, Saturn, Uranus, and Neptune too!

HEY...DID THE CAT SCRATCH YOU?
WELL, YOU KIND OF DESERVED IT!

HOIA BACIU FOREST

· ROMANIA ·
WEST OF THE CITY OF CLUJ-NAPOCA,
TRANSYLVANIA REGION
SIZE: 1.1 SQUARE MILES (3 SQ KM)

Did you know that there's a small forest on the northern border of Romania that, according to local legend, is home to UFOs (yep, them again), strange glowing lights, unexplained magnetic phenomena, ghosts, and other strange creatures, all at once? No?!
WELL, NOW YOU KNOW AND YOU CAN ALSO STOP SLEEPING SOUNDLY!

Hoia Baciu Forest is a very popular destination for hikers, sporty types, travelers, and tourists. But, in reality, it's the site of much more than one mystery!
Despite the fact that the forest is at least two centuries old, lots of the trees there seem to always be young and scrawny, as if they refuse to grow!
Plus, some clearings are perfectly, exactly circular: not a single blade of grass grows there, and no one knows why!

As if that weren't enough, many people say that people and animals have disappeared among its trunks over the years, and some even believe that the entire forest is home to the Devil!

So, sure, exploring the woods by bicycle is lovely...

BUT MAYBE, JUST IN THIS CASE, IT'S BETTER TO STAY HOME, PLANTED IN FRONT OF THE TV.

KRUDUM HILL

· CZECH REPUBLIC ·

KARLOVY VARY REGION, SLAVKOV FOREST

ELEVATION: 2,750 FEET (839 M) ABOVE SEA LEVEL

For your birthday, your parents gave you new hiking boots! You would rather have received action figures of your favorite superheros? TOO BAD! Because now you have to go for the nth hike up a hill!

KRUDUM HILL, COVERED IN NORWAY SPRUCE TREES, HAS HIDDEN TRULY JUICY LEGENDS FOR CENTURIES NOW. ESPECIALLY THOSE LINKED TO THE RUINS OF THE CHURCH OF SAINT NICHOLAS!

Located on a trade route between the Hungarian city of Eger and Prague, the church was super useful for the local villagers, pilgrims, merchants, and miners!
In 1253, it was donated to the Knights of the Cross with the Red Star. But over time, due to the closure of the mines and the Thirty Years' War (which was a bit of a headache for 17th-century Europe), everyone forgot about it!

SINCE THEN, STORIES OF ALL TYPES HAVE BEEN TOLD. LIKE HOW THE GHOSTS OF MINERS GO TO MASS, OR THAT THERE'S A MIGHTY TREASURE HIDDEN IN ITS RUINS!
It seems as though a Celtic stone was once found with writing that pointed to a place to dig...
But then it disappeared!

Have fun treasure hunters!

BUDA CASTLE LABYRINTH

· HUNGARY ·

City of Budapest – Length: 2 miles (3.3 km) – Depth: 40 to 50 feet (12 to 16 m)

When they took you on a field trip to Buda Castle, you probably didn't expect to be standing in front of what might just be the most famous GOTHIC building from the late Middle Ages, where the Hungarian emperors spent a lot of time showing everyone how important they were! But what we are really interested in isn't above: IT'S BELOW!

In the twists and turns of the south side of Castle Hill, in fact, is the Budavári Labirintus, a contorted set of tunnels, underground galleries, and offshoots that would make even a ghost lose his way!
Basically, it's a dark labyrinth filled with haze and musty air!
Just think: these miles-long underground caves were formed millions of years ago and were first inhabited by early humans!

They've seen it all over the years, being used as fire shelters, fully stocked wine cellars, food storerooms, hiding places for mysterious, precious treasure, Turkish harems, World War II hospitals... You name it!

For more than a decade, they were also the "vacation home" of a very important guest: Vlad III. This nobleman and warlord enjoyed impaling those who brought him lukewarm coffee. He was the inspiration for Count Dracula!

Did I say "Vacation home"? Oh, sorry, I meant "Prison where he was tortured."

DARGAVS

· RUSSIA ·
REPUBLIC OF NORTH OSSETIA-ALANIA
NEAR THE GIZELDON RIVER

Nestled amid the isolated clearings and mountains of Ossetia, there's a place
that looks like something out of a FAIRY TALE,
though it's actually very scary!
**WHY? WELL, BECAUSE IT CONSISTS OF LOTS OF ADORABLE LITTLE HOUSES....
FULL OF SKELETONS! INDEED, NEAR THE VILLAGE OF DARGAVS IS A NECROPOLIS
CALLED THE "CITY OF THE DEAD," BUILT BY THE OSSETIANS,
AN ANCIENT PERSIAN ETHNIC GROUPS.**

It's composed of a whopping 99 tombs and crypts up to four stories high,
and it seems that the oldest one dates back to the 12th century! Built in the
quintessential Nakh style, these stone block masonry structures have square
"windows" that hold the deceased. At the highest point, there's a tower from
which to watch over the dead. Heaven forbid they decide to take a walk to
stretch out their legs! According to local legend, those who enter
the cemetery won't come out alive!

*A STORY TO WARD OFF GRAVE ROBBERS...OR IS THERE
SOME TRUTH TO IT? IF YOU'RE BRAVE ENOUGH TO TRY,
BE MY GUEST!*

MAMMOTH BONE BUILDINGS

· UKRAINE AND RUSSIA ·
UKRAINE AND THE STEPPES OF WESTERN RUSSIA

Now that you're a BONE enthusiast, do you dream of making models of your favorites in your room? Wait 'til you hear about this one—no human bones this time! We're talking about...MAMMOTH BONES! **FROM ABOUT 23,000 TO 18,000 YEARS AGO, OUR ANCESTORS LIVED WITH SOME REALLY COLD WEATHER, THAT IS, THE LAST ICE AGE! IT WAS SO COLD, IT REACHED TEMPERATURES OF -4°F (-20°C) OR LOWER, AND NO, THERE WEREN'T ANY HEATERS OR COMFORTERS TO KEEP YOU WARM AT NIGHT.** Out and about, looking for shelter and water, there were also a lot of mammoths. So, primitive men thought:
"Look how big they are! We could build houses or something else with those bones!"

And so it was! Near the small village of Kostenki, Russia, the largest circular structure of all was recently found, consisting of 51 jaw bones and 64 skulls... from mammoths!

THE PROBLEM IS THAT NO ONE KNOWS WHAT IT WAS FOR! WAS IT A HOME? A PANTRY? A PLACE FOR RITUALS?

But it isn't the only one! In the entire area (also in Ukraine), at least 70 different such buildings have been found!

35

TUNNEL OF LOVE

· UKRAINE ·

Hamlet of Klevan, Rivne Oblast

Length: about 3 miles (5 km)

You're now walking on a railway track surrounded by green archways, bushes, and colorful leaves!

A TRAIN COULD SPEED DOWN THE TRACK AT ANY MOMENT, BUT YOU AREN'T AFRAID: THIS PLACE IS SIMPLY TOO BEAUTIFUL TO WORRY ABOUT THAT! YOU ARE IN THE TUNNEL OF LOVE, ONE OF THE MOST ROMANTIC AND MYSTERIOUS PLACES IN THE WORLD!

Located on the Kovel-Rivne line, this railway connects the hamlet of Klevan to a factory in the northern part of Orzhiv, allowing trains to transport woodworking materials three or four times a day! All it took was trains passing through the woods for decades to SHAPE the vegetation around them. The trees kept growing higher and higher, and the branches then extended over the top, just above the top of the train. The result is a truly magnificent sight!

ACCORDING TO LEGEND, THE TRACK WAS CREATED BY A YOUNG POLISH CATHOLIC ENGINEER FROM ORZHIV AS A DISPLAY OF HIS LOVE FOR AN ORTHODOX GIRL FROM KLEVAN, DESPITE THE OPPOSITION OF HER PARENTS. ISN'T THAT ROMANTIC?

But other people say that, during the Soviet era, trees were purposely planted so close to each other that they would conceal the transport of military armaments!

OKAY, THAT'S A LITTLE LESS ROMANTIC... BUT WHO KNOWS!

37

PAMUKKALE THERMAL POOLS

· TURKEY ·

Denizli Region, Southwestern Turkey
Surface Area: 4 square miles (10.4 sq km)

You have been feeling your way along for several feet by now, completely blinded by a light from an unknown source. You feel like you're in a desert...an ALL-WHITE desert! You come across a spring full of submerged ancient columns and take a sip of the water... YUCK! It's hot! Don't worry, you aren't hallucinating. It's just that you've ended up in the Pamukkale Thermal Pools! **Not far from the ancient city of Hierapolis, these pools are one of the oldest hot springs in the world. Throughout the centuries, they were used by doctors and healers for their patients (and they certainly took a dip in them too).**

The Turkish word "Pamukkale" means COTTON CASTLE, and the pools were so named because of their gleaming white surface, the product of calcite springs that have dripped down the surrounding mountainside for thousands and thousands of years. **The result is shimmering, slippery tubs upon tubs of hot mineralized water of at least 97°F (36°C).**

What about those underwater columns? Well, they belong to Cleopatra's Pool, which, according to legend, was built by the Roman Mark Antony for his beloved and very powerful Egyptian queen!

A powerful earthquake during Nero's rule caused them to collapse and sink, making the pools even more mysterious!

GIZA NECROPOLIS

· EGYPT ·

Giza Plateau, 15 Miles (25 km) from Cairo

Built Between 2575 and 2465 BCE

In ancient Egypt, pharaohs were powerful kings who were thought to be GODS on Earth! They were spoiled as can be from birth, only to be embalmed and entombed in sarcophagi full of useful items for the afterlife. And, since it was nothing to them, some of them said:

"For my funeral, I want to be buried in a very tall, strapping monument full of riches! Find 100,000 craftsmen, on the double!"

Thus the Giza Necropolis was born. One of the Seven Wonders of the World, it is composed of the three great pyramids of the pharaohs Khufu, Khafre, and Menkaure—and the Sphinx of course.
So, is that it?
No! It's actually full of mysteries! Such as: the missing mummies of the pharaohs, the alignment of the pyramids with Orion's Belt, and the method used to transport millions of blocks weighing tons to the site.

So, is the face of the Sphinx really that of Khafre? And is it true that a secret library full of papyri with the history of Atlantis is hidden under that giant feline?
Not to mention that many people think the ancient Egyptians got a few tips from...that's right! Aliens!

But let's move on...

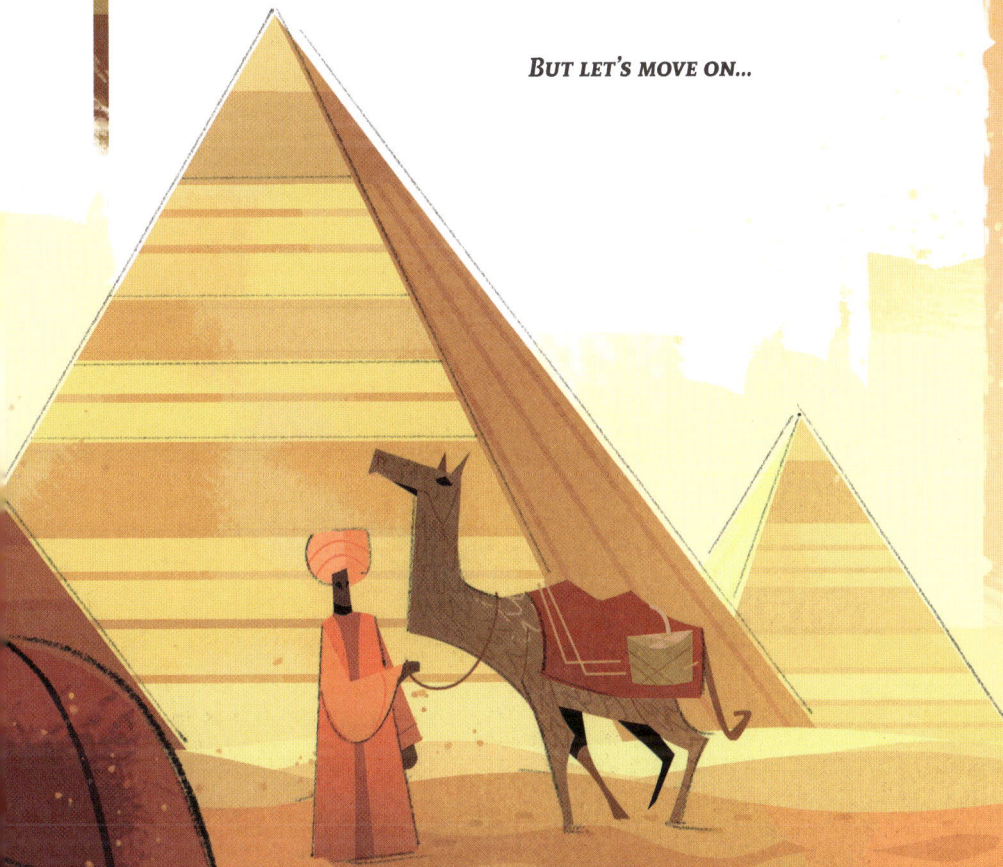

EYE OF THE SAHARA

· MAURITANIA ·
Sahara Desert, Near the City of Ouadane
Diameter: 25 miles (40 km)

For hours, you've been under the blazing Sahara sun on the back of a wobbly camel. Your bum really hurts, but finally, in the middle of the golden sand of the desert, you see it... A HOLE!

It isn't any old hole...

You're standing in front of the Richat Structure, also called the Eye of the Sahara!

Located in the Adrar plateau, it's an eroded dome that is divided into concentric rings formed by different types of colorful rock. A Willy Wonka factory for every rock collector worthy of the name!

How did it get this strange form? Well, that's simple: rocks don't all erode at the same speed and way. So, in the end, the result is a bit crazy in terms of shapes and colors!

At first, people thought it was the crater of a giant meteorite,
and they asked astronauts to check on it from outer space!

But today, people think that it all began around 100 million years ago, when the
Pangea mega continent was breaking up. That pushed a lot of magma upward and
formed a dome that then opened up after a second eruption (sort of like a zit).
DECADES OF EROSION THEN SHAPED THE EYE AS WE KNOW IT!

SURE, SOME PEOPLE SAY IT LOOKS JUST LIKE
PLATO'S DESCRIPTION OF THE LOST CITY OF
ATLANTIS... BUT LET'S MOVE ON!

FAIRY CIRCLES

EASTERN EDGE OF THE NAMIB DESERT
DIAMETER: 10 TO 65 FEET (3 TO 20 M)

They almost look like doodles on a notebook.
Or on your homework when you don't know the answer. But here, you certainly aren't
at school! First, there are no teachers (woo-hoo!). Second, you're surrounded by thousands
of strange RINGS of Stipagrostis grass without a single thing at their center!

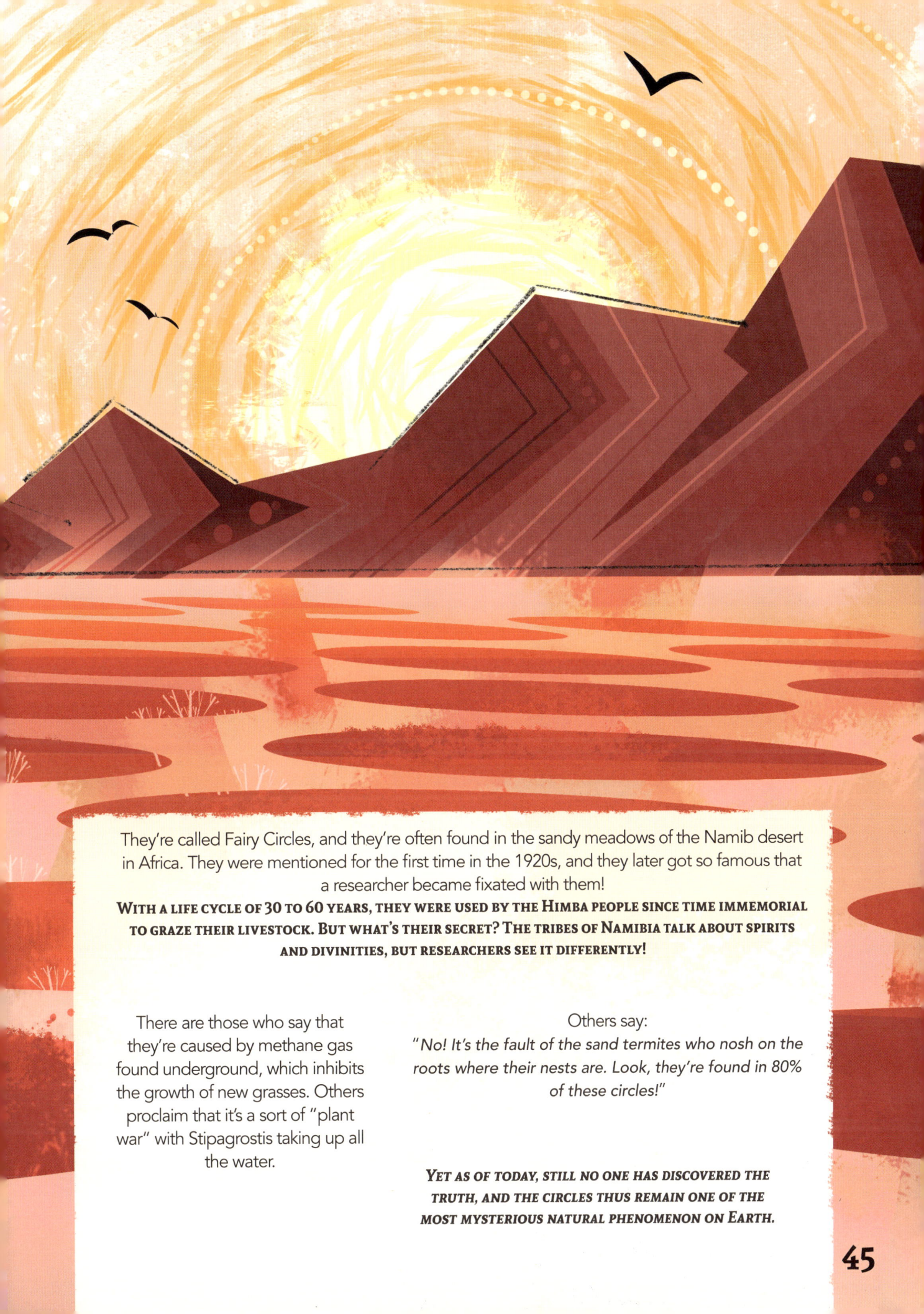

They're called Fairy Circles, and they're often found in the sandy meadows of the Namib desert in Africa. They were mentioned for the first time in the 1920s, and they later got so famous that a researcher became fixated with them!

WITH A LIFE CYCLE OF 30 TO 60 YEARS, THEY WERE USED BY THE HIMBA PEOPLE SINCE TIME IMMEMORIAL TO GRAZE THEIR LIVESTOCK. BUT WHAT'S THEIR SECRET? THE TRIBES OF NAMIBIA TALK ABOUT SPIRITS AND DIVINITIES, BUT RESEARCHERS SEE IT DIFFERENTLY!

There are those who say that they're caused by methane gas found underground, which inhibits the growth of new grasses. Others proclaim that it's a sort of "plant war" with Stipagrostis taking up all the water.

Others say:
"No! It's the fault of the sand termites who nosh on the roots where their nests are. Look, they're found in 80% of these circles!"

YET AS OF TODAY, STILL NO ONE HAS DISCOVERED THE TRUTH, AND THE CIRCLES THUS REMAIN ONE OF THE MOST MYSTERIOUS NATURAL PHENOMENON ON EARTH.

GATES OF HELL

· TURKMENISTAN ·

Near Darvaza Village, Ahal Province

Year of Creation: 1971

Did you know that there is a HUGE burning hole in the Karakum Desert where the flame never goes out? (No, this isn't an excuse to take a little trip and accidentally drop your homework into it.)

ALSO CALLED BY MANY OTHER NAMES, SUCH AS "DOOR TO HELL," THE GASEOUS CRATER OF DARVAZA HAS A DIAMETER OF ABOUT 230 FEET (70 M), IS AT LEAST 65 FEET (20 M) DEEP, AND HAS BEEN CONSTANTLY "ON" FOR MORE THAN 50 YEARS!

The whole area, in fact, is an endless deposit of natural gas and fossil fuel called Amu Darya, and decades ago geologists said:
"Come on! Let's dig a little bit here and a little bit there, we're sure to find oil!"

Too bad they got a little too carried away! The entire research facility collapsed to create a cavern filled with extremely toxic methane gas.
"Oh, no!" cried another researcher, trembling from head to toe.
"This gas might be dangerous! Let's create a fire, so it will burn off."
BUT EVEN TODAY, THE FIRE SEEMS TO SHOW NO SIGN OF STOPPING!

This perennial bonfire has also given rise to a lot of legends: it is said that it was actually caused by a meteorite, that spiders throw themselves into the crater for mysterious reasons, and that the gases come straight from Hell!

SMALL NOTE: THIS SITE ISN'T RECOMMENDED FOR THOSE WHO LIKE COOL WINTER WEATHER.

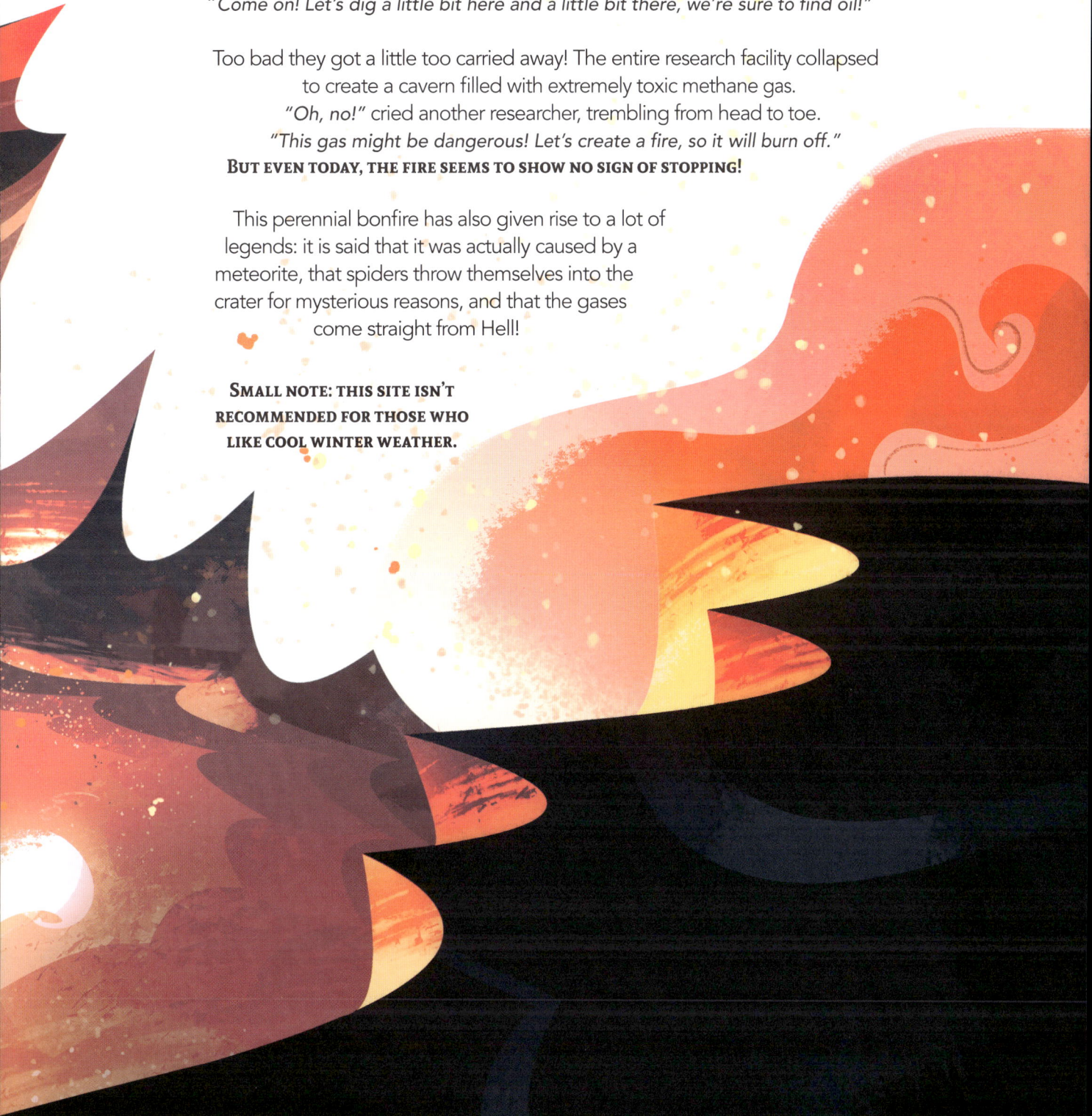

VAITHEESWARAN KOIL

· INDIA ·
State of Tamil Nadu
Construction: 11th century

You've seen it all and faced every mysterious journey imaginable, except one:
that of discovering your FUTURE!
No, I didn't binge on ice cream and then daydream about it. It really is possible!
Only you have to travel very far away.
All the way to INDIA.

VAITHEESWARAN KOIL (TRY SAYING THAT FIVE TIMES FAST) IS A HINDU TEMPLE DEDICATED
TO THE DEITY SHIVA, A POWERHOUSE WHEN IT COMES TO HEALING. IN FACT, THERE ARE
NECTAR-INFUSED WATERS IN THE TEMPLE TO CURE DISEASES
AND EVEN A SACRED MEDICINAL NEEM TREE.
But wait, there's more!

Nadi Astrology is also practiced within its walls. This involves predicting the future through the application of lots of dried palm leaves!

ACCORDING TO LEGEND, SEVEN SAGES RECEIVED DIVINE KNOWLEDGE ABOUT THE DESTINY OF ALL PEOPLE ON THE FACE OF THE EARTH (EVEN THOSE NOT YET BORN), AND THEN WENT AROUND TELLING PEOPLE ABOUT IT! THEIR VISIONS WERE PASSED DOWN ORALLY FOR THOUSANDS OF YEARS BEFORE THEY WERE WRITTEN ON LEAVES, IN SANSKRIT!

Family, success, love, health, you name it! Once you find the right leaf, after a long ritual and an even longer analysis by the temple's leaf readers, you can learn all about your future.

I DON'T KNOW IF THEY'LL BE ABLE TO TELL YOU YOUR NEXT GRADE IN MATH. BUT I CERTAINLY WON'T STOP YOU FROM TRYING!

NORTH SENTINEL ISLAND

· INDIA ·

Andaman Archipelago, Bay of Bengal – Surface Area: About 23 square miles (60 sq km)

So far you have been unlucky with the mystery islands, but let's give it one last try! The small island you are on is essentially paradise, with a narrow strip of beach surrounded by small coral reefs and barrier reefs, with a large forest in the middle of the island. It really is the perfect place to sit back and relax! Look, there's even a flock of diving birds! No, wait, those aren't birds... Those are arrows ready to pierce you! RUN!!!

That's right, you're on the island of North Sentinel, inhabited by about 50 or 500 Sentinelese, one of the most isolated tribes in the world. Completely ignored by the rest of civilization for at least 55,000 years, going back at least to the time of the first great prehistoric migration out of Africa!

So, no, they don't have TV or video games! We know very little about them. For example, we know that they fish, that they build small boats and huts, and they pick fruit! Over the centuries, there has been no way to learn more about them because as soon as anyone (whether researcher, explorer, or just a curious observer) tries to approach the island, they are immediately attacked with arrows and stone axes! Friendly contact has happened on rare occasions, but then the Indian government said: *"Whatever. Let's leave them alone for a while, OK?!"* And now it's illegal to get too close.

That's probably because they are also one of the most vulnerable tribes in the world: a simple cold would be enough to wipe them out completely!

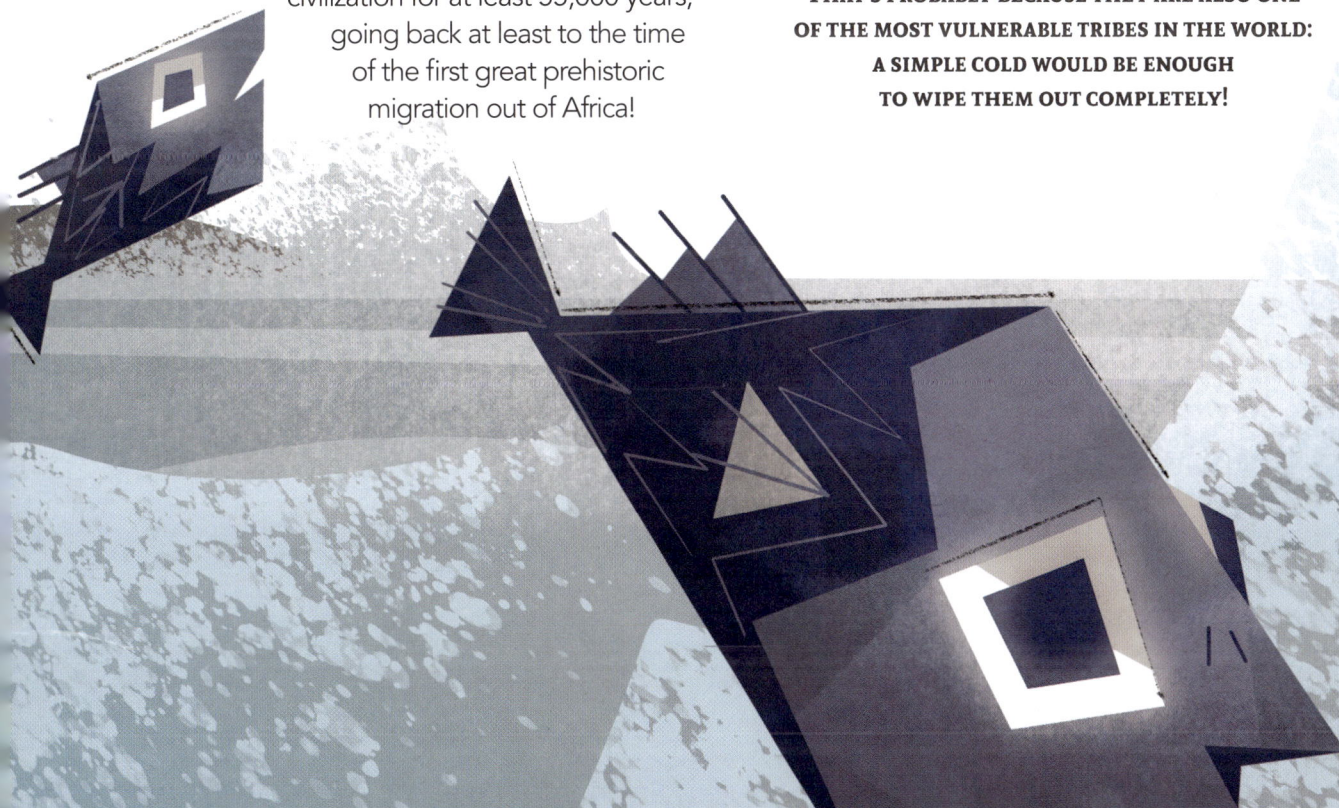

51

HEIZHUGOU FOREST

· CHINA ·
Sichuan Province, Leshan City-Prefecture
Surface area: About 325 square miles (838 sq km)

There's a sort of Bermuda Triangle in the middle of a FOREST, can you believe it? No?! Well, it exists. And it's hidden by fog, tall bamboo and...pandas!

We're now in China, in what's know as "Death Valley," an immense ancient forest where a lot of strange things happen, like illogical celestial phenomena or crazy geological events! Since the early 1900s, it seems that everything just disappears from this forest: animals, objects, and even people!

And the fog is always so thick that researchers can't seem to explore the forest properly. At least 60 vehicles have vanished into thin air here (including planes).

"Surely some curse is to blame!" say the conspiracy theorists.

"Surely aliens are to blame!" another might reply.

A few people living in the area have even said that a huge bird in the shape of a two-headed dragon lives in this forest!
But the truth is, most likely, that when people disappeared into thin air, it was due to a geomagnetic anomaly at least 40 miles (60 km) long, capable of driving compasses and vehicles crazy.
Who knows? So, to be on the safe side, always look up.

Heaven forbid a huge dragon sneezes on your neck!

TERRACOTTA ARMY

·CHINA·
Near Xi'an City, Shaanxi Province
Created Between 246 and 206 BCE

Imagine you're at the beach and digging a hole in the sand to create a little lake or well. But instead of finding the usual chipped shell, you make one of the most important and mysterious ARCHAEOLOGICAL discoveries in history!

That's essentially what happened to Yang Zhifa and his brothers. On March 29, 1974, they were working the land to dig a well. Suddenly, one of their picks hit something odd! What did they find? Not 1, not 2, not 3, but 8,000 soldiers, 130 wagons with 520 horses, and more than 100 cavalry horses!
All in clay!
It was the Terracotta Army of Qin Shi Huang, the first emperor of China. He was the sort of guy who didn't do much in life, you know, all he did was erect the Great Wall of China! Huang may have been a bit self-centered, so he ordered 700,000 workers to build him an entire life-size (yet fake) army for his grave!

Why, you ask? To conquer the world of the dead, or maybe to have company in the afterlife. He wouldn't want to get lonely! The soldiers vary in height depending on their rank, and they're extremely realistic in every detail, with different faces for each statue.

Originally, they were decorated with precious stones and painted with dyes made from cooked bones, tree sap, and a lot of other ingredients!

Take that, little chipped shell!

GENGHIS KHAN'S GRAVE

· MONGOLIA ·
UNKNOWN LOCATION
CREATION: 1227

You've been wandering through the endless clearings of Mongolia for days. "*But my friend told me it was right here!*" you think, in despair. "*Or maybe it was a little to the right, or maybe a little to the left?*" It's pointless. They've been pulling your leg and now you have to take the bus home, spending all your allowance. Sheesh! You've been looking for the burial site of the great leader Genghis Khan and, oops...NO ONE knows where it is!

GENGHIS KHAN NOT ONLY UNITED ALL THE MONGOL AND TURKIC TRIBES; HE ALSO CREATED THE LARGEST EMPIRE IN HUMAN HISTORY.
FROM SIBERIA TO PERSIA, FROM CHINA TO THE MIDDLE EAST!
SOME SAW HIM AS A CONQUEST-HUNGRY DESTROYER, AND OTHERS SAW HIM AS A HERO CAPABLE OF BRINGING PEACE AND CIVILIZATION!

The fact is that, at one point, he said, "*That's enough! I'm tired of all this attention. When I die, don't tell anyone where I'm buried!*" And so it was!
ACCORDING TO LEGEND, HIS BODY WAS TAKEN TO MONGOLIA BY A MOURNING ARMY, WHICH, WHILE IT WAS THERE, SKEWERED ANYONE IT ENCOUNTERED ALONG THE WAY. THEN THEY HAD THE GRAVE TRAMPLED BY A THOUSAND HORSES TO COVER EVERY TRACE.

SOME SAY HE'S IN BURKHAN KHALDUN, A SACRED MOUNTAIN IN KHENTII PROVINCE, WHERE HE WAS BORN. BUT SO FAR, NO ONE HAS BEEN ABLE TO FIND HIM, MAKING HIS GRAVE ONE OF THE MOST MYSTERIOUS PLACES IN THE WORLD!

MYSTERIOUS ROAD

· SOUTH KOREA ·
North-Central Jeju Island

Imagine you are driving with your family. The car window is open,
the air is ruffling your hair, and a rock song is playing in the background on the radio.
All of a sudden, PUFF PUFF PUFF,
the car breaks down right near a hill.
You don't even have time to dry the drink you spilled on your pants,
when the car starts moving on its own...
and going uphill!

Don't worry, there is no witchcraft behind it. It's just that you're on Mysterious Road!

On Jeju Island, most famous for its lush natural vegetation and Dol Hareubang (stone figurines of elderly grandparents), there is a street, also known as Dokkaebi Road, that connects two of the main highways and is located on a hill at the foot of a large mountain. Sounds pretty normal, right? Well, if you travel from south to north and, at some point, turn off the car, it will start going uphill on its own!

**GHOSTS? ALIENS? STRANGE MAGNETIC FIELDS? NO!
IT'S JUST AN OPTICAL ILLUSION!**

The road is inclined 3 degrees downward, but the surrounding landscape is inclined 6 degrees downward.
That's why it looks as if the car rolling up the hill, but in reality, of course, it is rolling downhill.

*TO THE DELIGHT OF THOSE IN A HURRY
TO GET TO WORK!*

ISE SHRINE

· JAPAN ·
City of Ise, Mie Prefecture, Kansai Region
Foundation (According to Legend): 4 BCE

You know when you construct a building with toy bricks and, after a while, you don't like it anymore and you decide to tear it down and start over again? Well, that's what happens in Japan...but with temples!

The Ise Shrine (also called Jingū) is a complex of many Shinto shrines. There are at least 125 of them in the entire area (who knows how many bricks you need to build them all), and more than 1,000 rituals are performed there every year. They're mostly dedicated to the worship of the sun goddess Amaterasu!

The problem is that practically NO ONE can go inside, except priests and members of the royal family! You, yes you, walking amid the surrounding groves as you nibble on a sandwich, at most, you can see a few thatched roofs behind the wooden fences!

And that's not all! Every 20 years, the temples are destroyed and rebuilt from scratch in the same style, so as to keep them unchanged over the centuries and maintain a kind of divine prestige.

Is that it? Absolutely not! Wait, I lost count of the mysteries!

The Ise Shrine complex is supposedly home to the Sacred Mirror, a bronze mirror symbolizing honesty and wisdom that is also one of the three sacred imperial treasures.

Too bad it's impossible to prove it: this object has never been seen or photographed!

PLAIN OF JARS

· LAOS ·
Xiangkhouang Province
Northern Edge of the Annamite Range
Creation: Estimated Between 500 BCE and 500 CE

The other morning, they told you about a fantastic place where very tall and very powerful GIANTS live, ruled by a king named Khun Cheung, who, after an important victory, had giant cups built from which to down drinks of all kinds!

I can tell you're skeptical!
"Giants?! That's impossible!
No one mentioned it on TV!"

So, you set out for that mysterious land but found no trace of these supposed giants. All that you saw was giant pots. Or, perhaps, those were their enormous cups?

You have reached the Thong Hai Hin, the Plain of Jars, a place filled with just that: cylindrical sandstone jars, between 1.6 and 13 feet (50 cm and 4 m) high!
Discovered only in 1909, the first digs were coordinated by an archaeologist named Madeleine Colani, who made a sensational discovery: the jars weren't used for food or drink, but as urns! That is, they contained the ashes of the dead.

In fact, they even found a cave in the center of the plain used as a crematorium, complete with holes on top that functioned as a chimney.
And, of course, there are plenty of wild legends about this place. Some locals think that the jars aren't carved out of stone but built from natural elements such as clay or sugar. Others say that dozens of ghosts roam the plain at night!

IN ANY CASE, EVEN TODAY, NO ONE KNOWS WHERE THEY REALLY CAME FROM!

CHEERS!
TO OUR HEALTH!

MARINE BIOLUMINESCENCE

· MALDIVES ·
MOST OF THE MALDIVES, BUT ESPECIALLY ON VAADHOO ISLAND, HUVADHU ATOLL

White sand, coral reefs, crystal-clear water, lots of swimming and diving every day. Perhaps you have FINALLY found the perfect island for a bit of R&R. And at night, everything is even more enchanting! Look at the moon, look at the...bright stars on the sand!?

DON'T WORRY. THIS TIME YOU'VE HIT THE JACKPOT. THERE ARE NO UNEXPLAINED EVENTS, ALIENS, OR UPSIDE-DOWN SKIES, JUST A NATURAL (THOUGH RATHER MYSTERIOUS) PHENOMENON CALLED...MARINE BIOLUMINESCENCE!

Bioluminescence occurs when living organisms emit light. Put simply, they manage to generate luminous energy through special chemical reactions! Lots of animals use it to hunt, frighten others, or court a new mate.

What you're observing is a brilliant, enchanting, phosphorescent color that can only be seen at night in many places around the world, such as Puerto Rico, India, New Zealand, and Jamaica. **BUT IN THE MALDIVES, ESPECIALLY IN SUMMER, THE PHENOMENON IS CAUSED BY A MICROORGANISM CALLED PHYTOPLANKTON THAT IS WASHED UP ON THE BEACH BY THE WAVES, CREATING THIS WONDERFUL LIGHT SHOW!**

No one really knows just why phytoplankton light up like this, but many researchers in crisp, white lab coats think it happens when those tiny organisms collide with each other. Tossed about by the waves, they get so stressed that a reaction is triggered, turning them into tiny light bulbs.

SLOPE POINT

· NEW ZEALAND ·

15 MILES (24 KM) FROM THE VILLAGE OF WAIKAWA
AND 45 MILES (70 KM) FROM THE TOWN OF INVERCARGILL

Slope Point is the most isolated, wildest, and southernmost area in all of New Zealand.
It also happens to be one of the most enchanted and mysterious!
At Slope Point, thanks to its proximity to Antarctica (I'm cold just thinking about it),
the winds are so powerful and rough that the very few trees that have managed
to grow among the slopes have become tangled up with each other, all of them
bent to the north. It's as if they were going to fly away!
Sections upon sections upon sections of twisted, rickety, bent,
deformed trees dot the entire area.

**AND NO, THEY AREN'T SPECIAL TREES. THEY ARE EXACTLY THE SAME ONES
THAT YOU'D FIND WALKING AROUND THE REST OF NEW ZEALAND.**

ACCORDING TO LOCAL LORE, IT SEEMS THAT THE TREES WERE PLANTED LONG AGO BY SHEPHERDS TO FEED THEIR SHEEP AND TO HAVE, FROM TIME TO TIME, A SHELTER WHERE THEY COULD FIND RESPITE FROM THE ELEMENTS. IN FACT, THERE ARE A FEW SHACKS USED BY FARMERS OUT THERE AMID THE TREES!

Everything is so inhospitable that apparently only about 60 people live in the area! It's the perfect destination if you want to spend some time alone meditating...

AS LONG AS A GUST OF WIND DOESN'T BLOW YOU AWAY TO WHO KNOWS WHERE!

DEVIL'S SEA

· PACIFIC OCEAN ·
BETWEEN THE ISLANDS OF HONSHU, LUZON, AND GUAM
SIZE: 502,000 SQUARE MILES (1,300,000 SQ KM)

Also called the Dragon's Triangle, this area is the lesser-known cousin of the Bermuda Triangle. And cousins they sure are, considering how much they have in common! Sea dragons swallowing ships, devils living in cities on the seabed, and underwater EXTRATERRESTRIAL bases (again!).

EVERY TALE YOU CAN IMAGINE HAS BEEN TOLD TO EXPLAIN THE DISAPPEARANCE OF FISHING BOATS AND RESEARCH VESSELS HERE IN THE EARLY 1950s.

But, even in this ocean, the cause could be much less exciting: perhaps it's electromagnetic activities that jam on-board equipment or explosions of undersea volcanoes and harmful natural gases.

ANYWAY.
WHO WANTS TO GO FOR A SWIM?

MARIANA TRENCH

· PACIFIC OCEAN ·
Between the Mariana Islands, Japan, the Philippines, and New Guinea
Length: 1,580 miles (2,550 km) – Width: 43 miles (69 km)
Maximum Depth: 36,069 feet (10,994 m)

You know that feeling when your friends dare you to dive into the deep end of the pool, but you don't feel up to it and everyone starts giggling? Well, now you can get back at them by asking them to jump into the deepest "pool" of all: THE MARIANA TRENCH!
With a crescent shape and several undersea volcanoes, this trench is the deepest oceanic depression in the world, reaching nearly 7 miles (11 km) in the Challenger Deep (that's quite a dive!). Just to give you a bit of perspective: Mount Everest measures "just" 5.5 miles (8.8 km)!

Of course, a lot of adventurous people have organized expeditions with ships and bathyscaphe submersibles to find out what lurks down there. But to fully explore such a mysterious place, it will take many more years!
And that's not all! In its pitch-black abysses, there are also incredible, very odd life forms, such as transparent "ghost" fish, alien-like shrimp, and so on.

One legend has it that a megalodon (a prehistoric shark that's 60 feet long with a 6.5-foot jaw) is also hiding down there.

ABRAHAM LAKE

· CANADA ·
NORTH SASKATCHEWAN RIVER, PROVINCE OF ALBERTA
SURFACE AREA: 20 SQUARE MILES (53.7 SQ KM)
LENGTH: 20 MILES (32 KM)

It looks like the enchanted landscape of an animated movie, or perhaps a CHEESY dream caused by too many snacks eaten late at night.

AND YET! YOU ARE WIDE AWAKE, AND ALSO VERY COLD! IN FACT, YOU ARE ON THE SHORE OF ABRAHAM LAKE, WHICH, EVERY WINTER, TEEMS WITH LARGE BUBBLES TRAPPED IN ICE!

Created in 1972 while the Bighorn Dam was being rebuilt, it has numerous plants on the seabed that, as they decompose, create methane bubbles that freeze just below the lake's surface.

THESE MYSTERIOUS GAS SCULPTURES ACCUMULATE UNTIL THEY APPEAR LIKE ROUNDED COLUMNS: A TRUE DELIGHT FOR PHOTOGRAPHERS!

BUT BETTER NOT PLAY WITH IT: METHANE IS HIGHLY FLAMMABLE!

BERMUDA TRIANGLE

· ATLANTIC OCEAN ·
BETWEEN MIAMI (FLORIDA), PUERTO RICO, AND THE BERMUDA ARCHIPELAGO
SIZE: 500,000 SQUARE MILES (1,100,000 SQ KM)

In 1840, the merchant ship *Rosalie* was found adrift, in perfect condition
but without a crew. The sole survivor? A CANARY in its cage!

THIS IS ONE OF THE CHILLING STORIES ABOUT THIS TWILIGHT ZONE WHERE SHIPS
AND PLANES HAVE "DISAPPEARED" FROM THE 1800S TO THE PRESENT!

Writer Charles Berlitz believed UFOs were to blame (them again?!),
irked that humans were crossing "their" flight zone.
Others have pointed a finger at sea monsters, a portal to another dimension,
and fiery rays cast from the legendary sunken city of Atlantis!

THE TRUTH IS THAT IT'S PROBABLY ALL CAUSED BY STORMS,
HUMAN ERROR, OR BAD LUCK...

BUT THAT'S
ANOTHER STORY!

AREA 51

· USA ·
Nevada Desert, 125 Miles (200 km)
from Las Vegas
Built: 1955

3,14

1,618

If you go for a walk on the Extraterrestrial Highway (remember your sunscreen), between miles 29 and 30 you'll come across a dirt road in the middle of nowhere. Beads of sweat, your favorite shoes covered in dust, no cell phone reception, and maybe you've seen a strange flying object. **DON'T WORRY, YOU AREN'T IMAGINING THINGS. YOU JUST HAPPEN TO BE STANDING NEAR AN AIR BASE THAT HAS MANY NAMES, BUT ONE IS THE MOST FAMOUS OF ALL: AREA 51.**

The military used this remote place for nuclear testing before converting it into a development and testing facility for super-fast spy planes during the Cold War. All of it top secret, of course. That was until 1989, when a certain Robert Lazar let it slip on TV that ALIEN TECHNOLOGY was being studied there. Since then, the base has become a playground for conspiracy theorists: laser guns, the flying saucer that crashed at Roswell in 1947, aliens and humans having coffee together and commenting on football games.

THE RUMORS HAVE BEEN DEBUNKED, BUT TO THIS DAY, NO ONE KNOWS WHAT IS REALLY GOING ON THERE.

IT'S A MYSTERIOUS PLACE THAT CONTINUES TO DRAW TOURISTS, THEMED FESTIVALS, AND PEOPLE DRESSED AS ALIENS EVERY YEAR.

SAILING STONES AT RACETRACK PLAYA

·USA·

Death Valley National Park, California
Documented for the First Time in 1948

You're starting to feel like you're being followed. Yet you're the only one out here! It's just a huge dry lake without a soul. So then...how come that rock isn't where it was before? And that one! And that one, too! Don't panic! Do those stones want to kidnap you!?

No, don't worry! It's just that you're right in the middle of Racetrack Playa, the only desert in the world where the rocks move by themselves! For decades, the movement of rocks has been one of Earth's greatest mysteries. Seeing boulders that weigh up to 660 pounds (300 kg) leave very long trails or zig-zag on their own isn't exactly an everyday occurrence!

Researchers here had fun, even giving funny names to the stones, while theorists of supernatural phenomena and UFOs were already sharpening their pencils.
But the truth is a bit like a simple recipe:

– 2.75 inches (7 cm) of rainwater need to freeze at night to create 3 to 6 mm ice sheets that leave stones uncovered.

– Then, wait for the morning sun's heat to break the ice into a bunch of small panels and add wind.

– The wind moves the ice sheets and, with them, the large, mysterious stones at a speed of about 3.3 feet (1 m) per second, generating the very famous tracks!

What a force of nature!

NAICA MINE

· MEXICO ·
MINING VILLAGE OF NAICA, STATE OF CHIHUAHUA
DEPTH: BETWEEN 400 AND 1,000 FEET (120 AND 300 M)

You might think you are in SUPERMAN'S Fortress of Solitude, where our hero takes naps after teaching villains a lesson, but you are sorely mistaken! You are actually 1,000 feet (300 m) underground, in the Cueva de los Cristales, surrounded by absolutely massive selenite crystals! Derived from the Greek word for "moon stones," these behemoths can reach 36 feet (11m) in height. They have been forming for as long as 26 million years, immersed in mineral-rich waters.

SISTER OF THE SMALLER CUEVA DE LAS ESPADAS DISCOVERED IN 1910 AT 400 FEET (120 M), THIS LARGER CRYSTAL CAVE WAS UNEARTHED IN 2000 BY TWO SIBLING MINERS AND DUBBED "THE CRYSTAL SISTINE CHAPEL." TOO BAD IT'S ALSO ONE OF THE MOST DANGEROUS PLACES ON EARTH!

With temperatures of up to 140°F (60°C) and 100% humidity, scholars must wear air-conditioned suits and respirators, otherwise they would be cooked to a crisp in under ten minutes flat!

FOR YEARS, ENORMOUS PUMPS EXTRACTED WATER FROM THE CAVES BEFORE BEING TURNED OFF SO THAT THE CRYSTALS COULD KEEP GROWING...

... SUBMERGING THE MINE IN MYSTERY ONCE AGAIN.

ISLAND OF THE DEAD DOLLS

· MEXICO ·
Tequila Lagoon, in the Xochimilco Canals
An hour and a half from the
Embarcadero Cuemanco

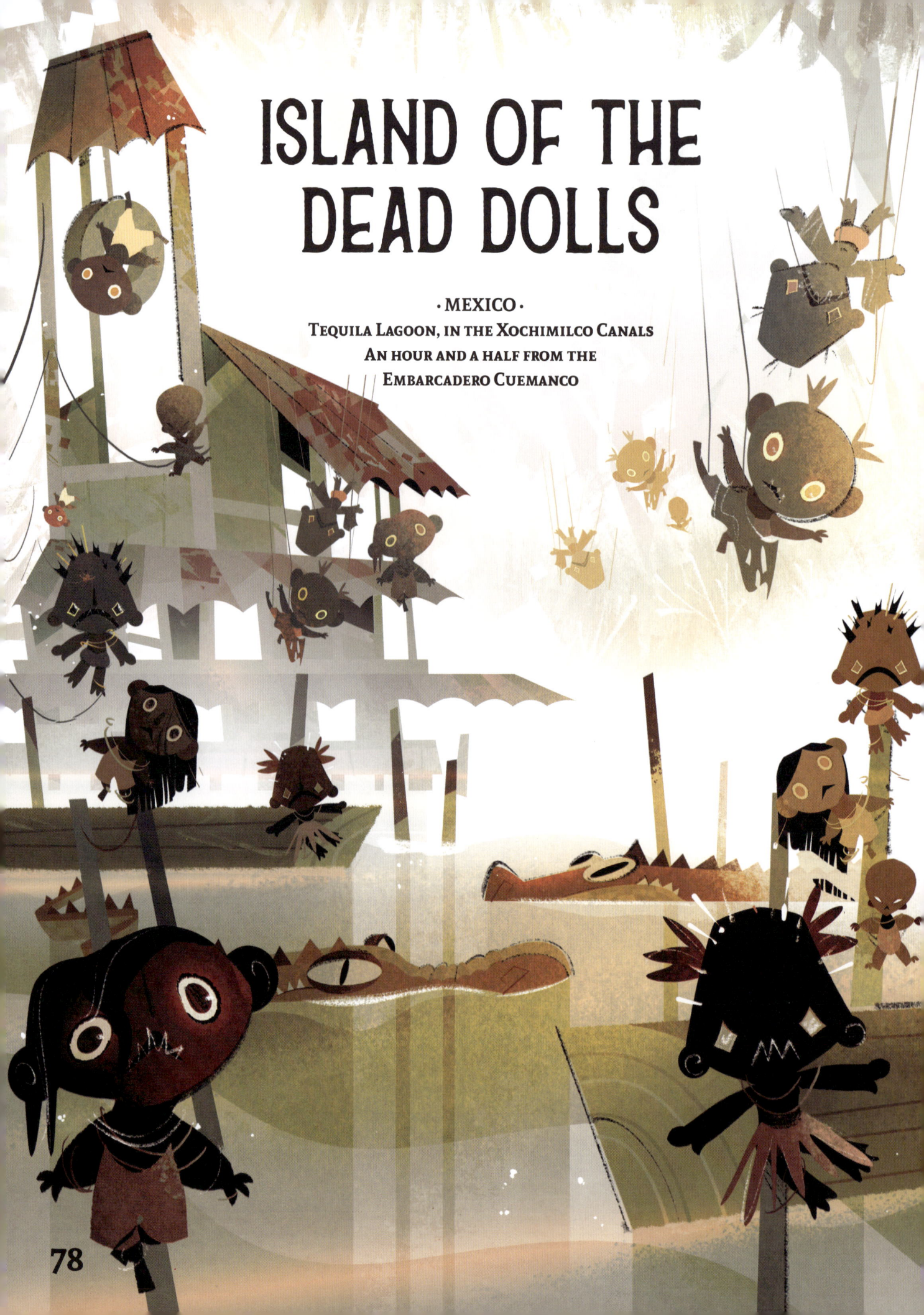

You are aboard a traditional local boat called a TRAJINERA, surrounded by a wild, lush lagoon. All around you are old *chinampas* (i.e., man-made islands used for farming) and a few colorful birds in the sky. But then you notice something hanging from a tree... Is it a doll?! **ACTUALLY, IT ISN'T JUST ONE! YOU BEGIN TO COUNT: ONE, TWO, FIVE, TEN... THERE ARE SO MANY OF THEM! THE ENTIRE ISLAND IS FULL OF DIRTY, UGLY, DUSTY OLD DOLLS, RIDDLED WITH COBWEBS AND OFTEN WITHOUT ARMS OR LEGS! IT SOUNDS LIKE ONE OF THOSE HORROR MOVIES YOU TRIED TO WATCH WITHOUT YOUR PARENTS FINDING OUT! EXCEPT THIS IS A REAL-LIFE ISLAND CALLED ISLA DE LAS MUÑECAS (ISLAND OF THE DOLLS). IT ONCE BELONGED TO DON JULIÁN SANTANA BARRERA, A FARMER, PREACHER, AND A BIT OF A HERMIT.**

The legend goes that he failed to save a young girl who was drowning in the water near his home, and the next day, he found a doll in the same spot where she had died (do you have goosebumps yet?). Feeling tormented by her vicious spirit, he decided to hang the doll from a tree, hoping to calm her down.

AND JUST TO BE EXTRA SURE, HE COLLECTED MORE AND MORE OF THEM, UNTIL HE HAD A COLLECTION OF THOUSANDS OF CREEPY DOLLS.

THE LOCALS EVEN BEGAN TO THINK THAT HE CULTIVATED THE LAND JUST TO FEED THEM!

In 2001, Barrera was found lifeless in the water. Right there, in the same spot where that girl had died years before...

SENDS SHIVERS DOWN YOUR SPINE, RIGHT?!

SNAKE ISLAND

· BRAZIL ·

22 MILES (35 KM) FROM THE CITY OF PERUÍBE, STATE OF SÃO PAULO
SIZE: 106 ACRES (43 HECTARES)

How great is summer, especially when spent on the idyllic shores of a tropical island? Crystal clear water, a fruit juice with a little umbrella stuck in it and...**THOUSANDS OF SNAKES!?** Seems like the travel agency messed up big time and sent you to the island of Queimada Grande, which has the lovely distinction of being populated by about 4,000 SNAKES. **IN SHORT, A HORROR MOVIE SET WHERE YOU WOULDN'T EVEN DREAM OF ABANDONING THE CLASSMATE WHO STOLE YOUR SNACK.**

It is ranked as one of the most dangerous uninhabited places in the world, partly because of its 2,000 golden lancehead pit vipers (help!). This type of viper is only found on this island and is considered a real superstar because of its **DEADLY VENOM**!

TODAY, FISHERMEN
ENJOY TELLING CHILLING
STORIES ABOUT THE ISLAND:
SOME SAY THAT IT'S AN ALIEN DEN
(THEM AGAIN!) AND OTHERS CLAIM THAT THE
SNAKES WERE RELEASED THERE BY PIRATES
TO PROTECT THEIR VALUABLE TREASURE!

WHO KNOWS?
FOR NOW, JUST WORRY ABOUT RUNNING FOR YOUR LIFE!

ENCHANTED WELL

· BRAZIL ·
Chapada Diamantina National Park, Near the Village of Andarai
Depth: 213 feet (65 m)

Would you like to visit a mysterious place without weird, dangerous surprises such as snakes, noisy lightning, twilight-zone seas, scary dolls, and ALIENS just for once?

All right, all right. This time I'll indulge you and take you to see the ultimate Enchanted well! Imagine that it's 1940 and you're a Brazilian hunter walking around looking for prey. All of a sudden, you come across a big crack in the ground.

And of course, you say to yourself: *"What a cool crack! Surely some animals are hiding in there. Wait till I tell my friends!"* Well... I don't want to be a killjoy, but there wasn't so much as a shadow of something to catch. Just a cave with a fairy-tale-like pool in it that had been a secret for thousands of years!

To get there, first you have do go down a long descent and then a path where it's best to hold on to special ropes (safety first!). But once you get there, you'll see why this grotto is famous: its intense, crystal-clear blue water makes it a truly enchanted place!

Between April and September, the light floods in and you can even see the pebbles on the bed of the pool clearly, at a depth of about 200 feet (60 m)!

Did you enjoy your vacation?
Good, but don't get too comfy.

Our next stop is a real thunderbolt!

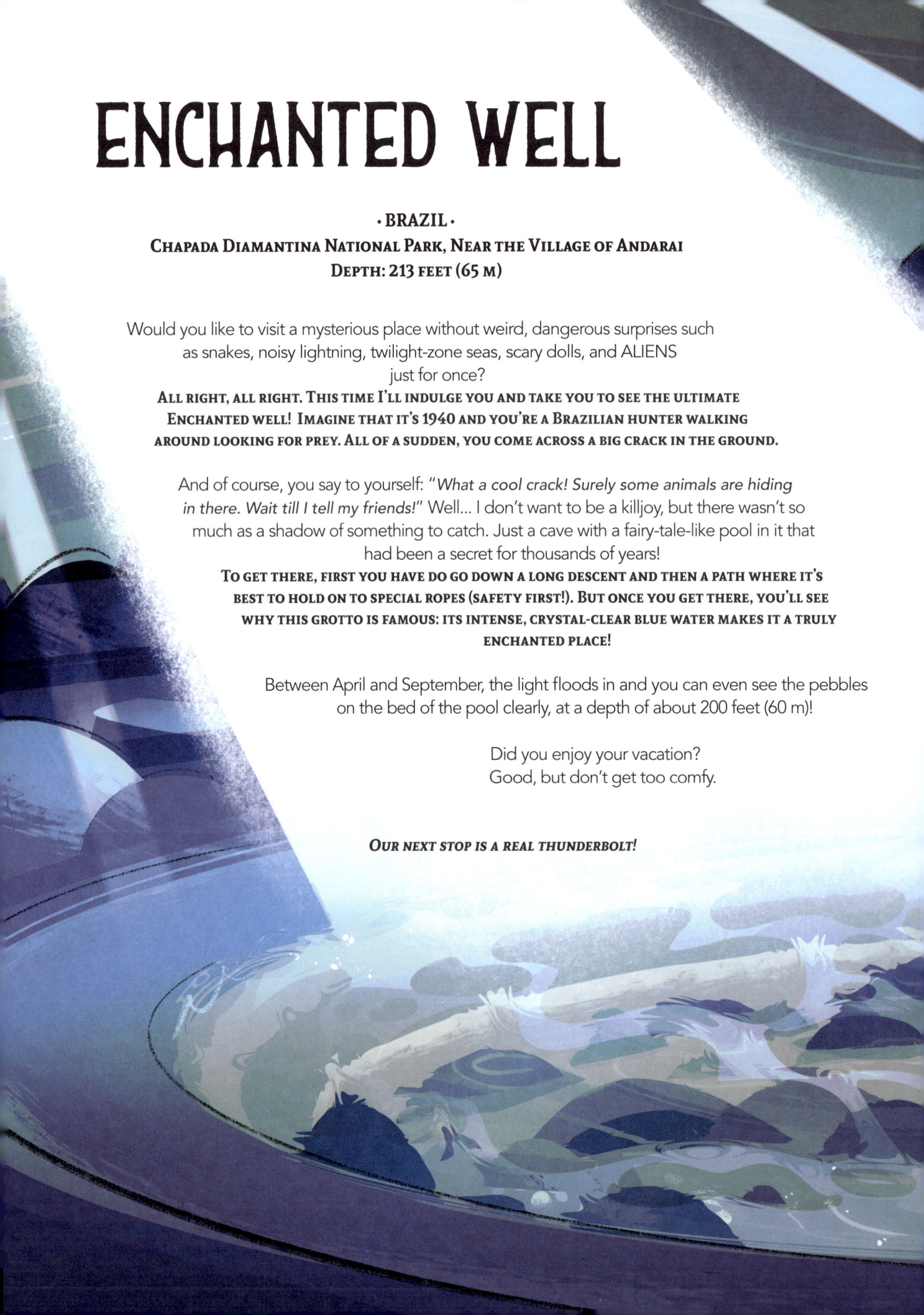

CATATUMBO LIGHTNING

· VENEZUELA ·
THE MOUTH OF THE CATATUMBO RIVER
SOUTH AND WEST WHERE IT FLOWS INTO
LAKE MARACAIBO

For 140 to 160 nights a year, a truly ELECTRIFYING event occurs (not in the sense of "exciting," but one that, if it hits you, will make your hair stand on end like a mad scientist): a cluster of storm clouds creates lightning for about 10 hours a day! Locally known as *El Relampago*, this phenomenon generates continuous lightning, most of it entirely within the clouds, visible up to hundreds of miles away!

IN SHORT: IMAGINE ABOUT 1,176,000 ELECTRICAL CHARGES PER YEAR WITH AN OVERALL INTENSITY AS HIGH AS 400,000 AMPS...

Power like that would completely turn the cheesy toast you were so lovingly preparing into dust. In 1841, the Italian geographer Agustín Codazzi described it as something capable of guiding sailors, sort of like a lighthouse. And, as it turns out, it has also been called the "Maracaibo Lighthouse" for centuries.

BUT HOW COME ALL THESE LIGHTNING BOLTS ARE UP THERE HAVING A PARTY? SIMPLE: STORMS ARISE FROM WINDS AS THEY BLOW CROSS THE LAKE AND INTO THE SURROUNDING MOUNTAIN RIDGES. MOISTURE AND HEAT GENERATE ELECTRICITY, AND WHEN THE AIR MASSES MEET THE MOUNTAINS, THEY DESTABILIZE, WITH A BANG! THOUGH THEY MAY LOOK IMPRESSIVE, THEY AREN'T THAT DANGEROUS.

IN FACT, AIRPLANES BOUND FOR MARACAIBO PASS THROUGH IT EVERY DAY AS IF IT WERE NOTHING!

UYUNI SALT FLAT

· BOLIVIA ·
LOCATED IN THE DANIEL CAMPOS PROVINCE, NEAR THE CITY OF UYUNI
SURFACE AREA: 4,085 SQUARE MILES (10,582 SQ KM)

For some time now, table salt as been flavorless to you.
It's been keeping you up at night: it's become your obsession!
You need something more adventurous to season your pasta with.
So you decide to go on a long trip, until you land smack-dab in front of a mirage full
of FLAMINGOS, cacti, islands, Inca ruins, and geysers at 12,000 feet (3,650 m) up.

**YOU'RE IN THE UYUNI SALT FLAT IN THE NORTHERN ANDEAN HIGH PLAINS,
THE LARGEST SALT FLAT ON THE PLANET!**
With its 10 billion metric tons of salt, the salt flat was part of a prehistoric salt lake
called Minchin, which, over time, has evaporated, forming two lakes and two salt deserts
(how many times have I mentioned salt?).

Salt (again!) covers everything with a few meters of crust, creating an almost perfectly flat
expanse that, when it's rainy season, reflects the sky and makes it seem as if local SUVs are
flying in the sky. There are lots of legends about this place!

**LIKE THAT OF TUNUPA, A BEAUTIFUL GIRL WHOSE DEFECT WAS MAKING ALL THE MEN FALL IN LOVE
WITH HER. JEALOUS, THE OTHER WOMEN DECIDED TO MAKE HER DAUGHTER DISAPPEAR, AND POOR
TUNUPA NEVER STOPPED CRYING, FLOODING THE FIELDS AND MAKING THE LAND BARREN:
A SALT DESERT WAS FORMED.**

*THE INCAS, ON THE OTHER HAND, BELIEVED THAT THE DESERT
CONCEALED THE OJOS DEL SALAR, ENORMOUS WELLS THAT
SWALLOWED UP ENTIRE CARAVANS!*

EL OJO, THE ROTATING ISLAND

· ARGENTINA ·
Paraná Delta, Province of Buenos Aires
Diameter: 387 feet (118 m)

After a healthy walk, you've decided to stop in a nice area for a picnic. But you don't even have time to take a bite of your sandwich when the land around you begins to move mysteriously, making YOUR HEAD SPIN!
You can say goodbye to your relaxing break, but at least now you know where you are! You're at El Ojo, the strange rotating island!

Meaning "the Eye," it's a small uninhabited circular island that is found within a freezing lake that's just a bit bigger. El Ojo is constantly spinning on its axis, making it seem like a curious eye that's looking all around!

The first satellite image is from 2003, but this circle of earth was brought to the fore not long after by Argentinian director Sergio Neuspiller, who was seeking out a place where he could film a movie about the paranormal.

When he discovered its existence, he shelved his old project to show, via a documentary, that El Ojo is...that's right, an alien base, a landing platform for UFOs and the like (again!).

SOME RESEARCHERS SAY THE ISLAND MOVES THANKS TO LARGE NATURAL WELLS THAT≠ CREATE FLOWING WATER. THIS MOVEMENT AND THE EROSION CAUSED BY COLD WATER ARE WHAT TURNED THE ISLAND INTO AN ALMOST PERFECT DISC.

IN ANY CASE, IT'S BEST TO ENJOY IT WHILE IT LASTS, BECAUSE EROSION MIGHT MAKE IT SMALLER AND SMALLER, UNTIL IT DISAPPEARS FOREVER.

NAZCA LINES

· PERU ·

Nazca Desert, Theoretically Between 300 BCE and 500 CE

Surface Area: 8,105/6,286 /7,534 square feet

(753/584/700 sq m)

After a long nap, you wake up hoping to enjoy your well-deserved vacation surrounded by palm trees and crystal clear water... Wrong! The travel agency must have messed up again and here you are on a plane in the middle of an arid plateau. Look down and what do you see? Lots and lots of DRAWINGS! No, not the kind your classmates scribble on your desk. These are geoglyphs created by the Nazca people in ancient times, perfectly preserved today thanks to the dry, windless climate!

THE LOCALS LOVED ART SO MUCH THAT, FOR CENTURIES, THEY CHURNED OUT 13,000 LINES AND MORE THAN 800 ANIMAL FIGURES, INCLUDING WHALES, PARROTS, HUMMINGBIRDS, MONKEYS, AND FRIENDS, FOR CENTURIES, SOME BETWEEN 150 AND 600 FEET (45 AND 180 M) LONG.

To get the job done, it seems they started with small-scale designs and then, climbing to the top of the nearby mountains, they enlarged them with ropes. Then they would sweep away the red pebbles from the surface of the Nazca Desert, leaving only the white sand exposed.

WERE THEY MESSAGES FOR THE GODS? DID THEY SERVE AS A SORT OF ASTRONOMICAL CALENDAR OR WERE THEY "SIGNS" TO MARK THE WAY FOR PILGRIMS? PERHAPS THEY WERE USED TO CARRY WATER TO THE FIELDS, OR MAYBE THEY WERE LANDING STRIPS FOR ALIEN SPACECRAFT (YES, YOU READ THAT CORRECTLY).

IN ANY CASE, ENJOY THE VIEW!

MACHU PICCHU

· PERU ·
Urubamba, Cusco Department
Picchu Gorge, Urubamba Province, Built Around 1440
Altitude: 7,972 feet (2,430 m)

You're walking through the Andes and the Amazon rain forest.
You're surrounded by mist, pristine jungles, breathtaking scenery,
and a llama who keeps glaring at you and probably thinks you need
to work out a bit more.

Basically, you're in Machu Picchu, the most symbolic city of the Inca Empire!

BUILT BY THE FIRST EMPEROR PACHACÚTEC BETWEEN TWO PEAKS AND ON THE VALLEY OF THE TURBULENT URUBAMBA RIVER, IT WAS INHABITED UNTIL THE SPANISH CONQUEST IN 1532, THEN ABANDONED AND FORGOTTEN FOR CENTURIES. IT WAS ONLY IN 1911 THAT HISTORIAN HIRAM BINGHAM BROUGHT IT TO THE WORLD'S ATTENTION ONCE AGAIN!

Somewhere between 300 and 1,000 people called the city home, all of them members of a SUPER-IMPORTANT, ELITE GROUP within the emperor's court. The city was divided into agricultural and urban areas with at least 172 buildings, including temples, homes, schools, and observatories. Many scholars see Machu Picchu as a kind of "winter home" for the ruler, eager to enjoy its mild climate, while others believe it was an important religious, astronomical, or military center.

BUT HOW DID THEY CONSTRUCT SUCH A COMPLICATED CITY WITHOUT IRON, STEEL, CONCRETE, OR WHEELS? AND WHY WAS IT ABANDONED, DESPITE THE FACT THAT THE CONQUISTADORS HAD ALMOST IGNORED THE ENTIRE AREA?

TOO BAD THE INCA HAD NO WRITTEN LANGUAGE AND NO ONE LEFT US A SECRET DIARY SO THAT WE COULD DISCOVER THE TRUTH!

EASTER ISLAND

· CHILE ·

Valparaíso Region, Pacific Ocean
Built Between 1250 and 1500 CE

The year is 1722 and you're cutting across the Pacific Ocean on your three Dutch sailing ships. You are Admiral Jacob Roggeveen, and between flavorless soups and yet another seasick cabin boy, you notice an island about 2,330 miles (3,750 km) off the Chilean coast.

"How beautiful! What do you want to call it?" exclaimed the cabin boy, all green in the face.

"Umm, well, today is Easter Sunday. Let's call it Easter Island!"

Once you disembark, you discover not only that it's inhabited by an indigenous population, but that the coasts are chock-full of MONOLITHIC HUMAN FIGURES that stand up to 30 feet (10 m) high and weigh up to 90 tons (80 metric tons).

WITH HUGE NOSES AND THICK EYEBROWS, THESE GRUMPY, LONG-FACED SCULPTURES NEVER SMILE!

Called Moai, they were created in the tuff quarries of the Rano Raraku volcano and the Puna Pau crater. They wear headdresses and loincloths, and often on their backs are inscriptions in Rongorongo, a still-undeciphered language.

THEY COULD REPRESENT ANCESTORS, CONTACT WITH HI-TECH ALIENS, OR ANCIENT LOCAL DEITIES.

ONE THING THAT EVERYONE AGREES ON IS THAT THEY BRING GOOD LUCK: IN FACT, THEY LOOK INWARD, TO THE ISLAND AND NOT THE OCEAN, TO PROTECT THE INHABITANTS!

95

ILLUSTRATOR

Illustrator Domenico Russo attended the animation course at the Nemo Academy in Florence, Italy, and the masterclass Stephen Silver Drawing Academy in Los Angeles. He made his debut as a concept artist and color artist in several Italian and international animated productions and then specialized in editorial illustration. He has designed illustrated books, including classics for children, illustrations for advertising, puzzle games, and trading cards. His graphic style is strongly inspired by the golden age of American illustration and brings his greatest passions to the stage: classical literature, folklore, and Southern Italy.

AUTHOR

Brian Freschi has worked in both theater and science, while most recently diving into the world of publishing by creating engaging realities for Italian and international youth. Freschi is already the author of several comics, published in multiple languages. He also teaches comic screenwriting at TheSign in Florence, Italy.

GRAPHIC DESIGN BY
Valentina Figus

WS whitestar kids™ is a trademark of White Star s.r.l.

© 2025 White Star s.r.l.
Piazzale Luigi Cadorna, 6 - 20123 Milan, Italy
www.whitestar.it

Translation: Katherine Kirby
Editing: Abby Young

First printing, August 2025

ISBN 978-88-544-2158-5
1 2 3 4 5 6   29 28 27 26 25

Printed and manufactured in China by
Shenzhen Dream Colour Printing Company Limited,
Shenzhen, Guangdong

FSC
www.fsc.org
MIX
Paper | Supporting
responsible forestry
FSC® C178000

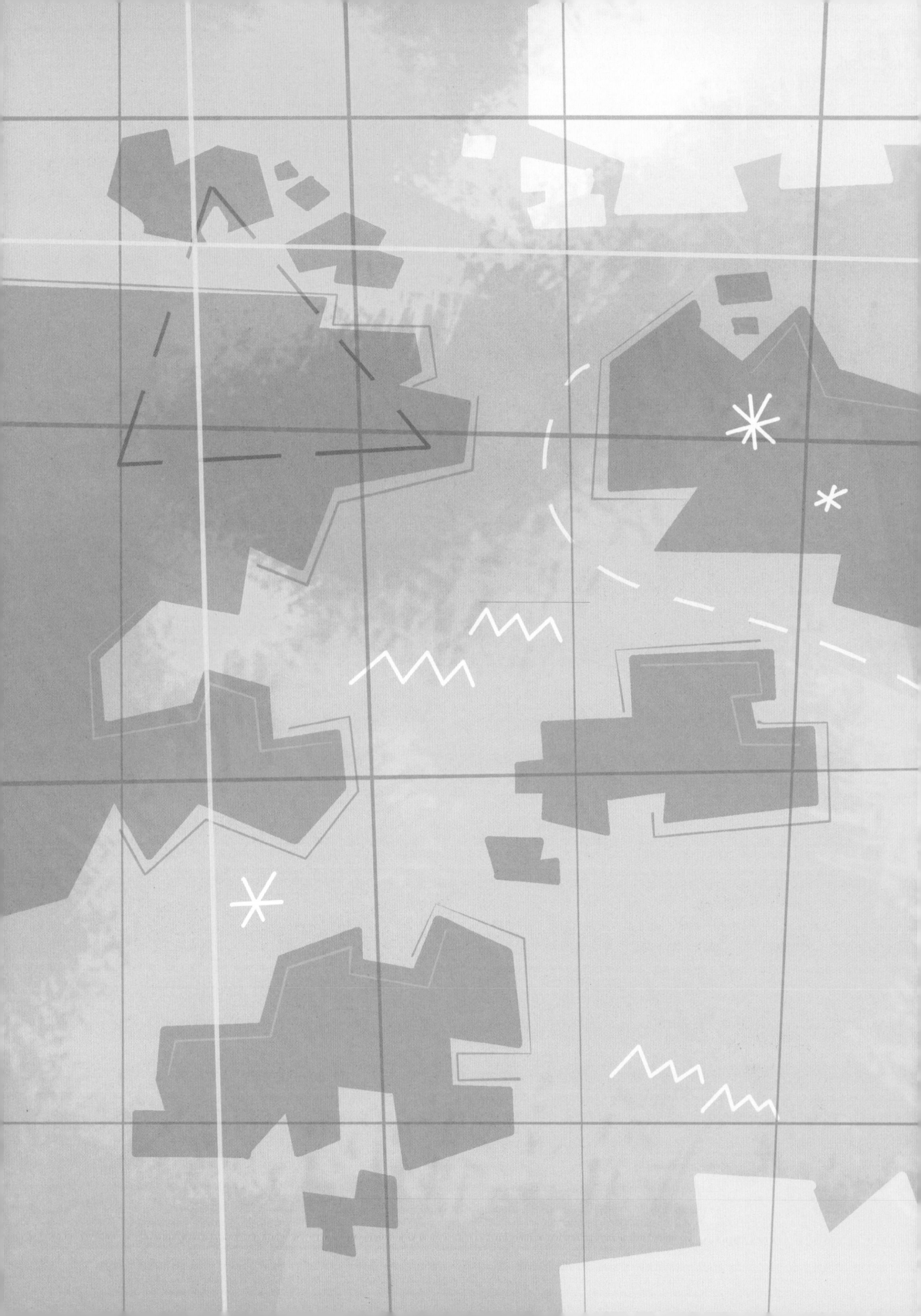